Management Buyouts

Management Buyouts

Success and Failure Away From
the Corporate Apron Strings

David Clutterbuck and Marion Devine

Hutchinson Business
London Melbourne Auckland Johannesburg

First published in 1987 by Hutchinson Business
An imprint of Century Hutchinson Ltd
62–65 Chandos Place, London WC2N 4NW

Century Hutchinson Australia (Pty) Ltd
PO Box 496, 16–22 Church Street, Hawthorn,
Victoria 3122, Australia

Century Hutchinson New Zealand Ltd
PO Box 40–086, 32–34 View Road, Glenfield,
Auckland 10, New Zealand

Century Hutchinson South Africa (Pty) Ltd
PO Box 337, Bergvlei 2012, South Africa

Phototypeset in 10/11 Helvetica
by Input Typesetting Ltd, London

Printed in Great Britain by
Redwood Burn Limited, Trowbridge, Wiltshire

British Library Cataloguing in Publication Data

Clutterbuck, David
Management buyouts.
1. Management buyouts—Great Britain
I. Title II. Devine, Marion
658.1′6 HD2746.6

ISBN 0–09–172270–5

Contents

Introduction

It all started in the United States. True, there had been occasional management buyouts in Britain, primarily by a retiring company founder with no suitable heir to receive the reins of management who wanted to see the company continue as before. But the sudden explosion of such deals and the general awareness of managers that they could become wealthy by acquiring the business they work for is a phenomenon that began in the late 1970s in the United States and spread rapidly to Europe in the early 1980s. In 1978 the Industrial and Commercial Finance Corporation ICFC (now Investors in Industry 3i) handled a mere 10 buyouts. In 1979 there were 20, in 1980 49, and in 1981 70. By 1986, there were at least 140 buyouts in the first six months alone.

Altogether there have been at least 1500 management buyouts in the UK in the past ten years and the number per annum is still rising. So, too, is the size of deals. In 1981, the Hornby buyout at £5.5 million was big news. By 1986, the largest recorded deal was the £173 million acquisition of Mardon Packaging (now Lawson Mardon) by its managers. (This still palls by comparison with some deals in the United States, such as the reported $4.2 billion buyout of Safeway Stores and the reported $3.5 billion buyout of the department store Macy.) The average deal value in the UK had risen from around £500,000 to £4 million between 1980 and 1985, according to the University of Nottingham's Centre for Management Buyouts. The 227 buyouts recorded by the Centre in 1985 were worth a total of £930 million. In addition, there was an unrecorded volume of buyouts financed by loan capital alone. Estimates for 1986 suggest that well over £1 billion was spent on buyouts.

The boom in buyouts looks set to continue for some years yet. 'There is an almost inexhaustible supply of these things', commented the managing director of Charterhouse Development, which claims to be the oldest venture capital group in Britain. According to Nottingham, two out of every three buyouts are in manufacturing. This is understandable, as manufacturing companies are more likely to have a solid asset base. However, buyouts have been recorded in most sectors.

Looked at another way, management buyouts now account for between one sixth and one third (depending on source of estimate) of all acquisitions in the UK, compared with just 3 per cent in 1977.

So just what is a management buyout? This is how accountants Spicer and Pegler define it: 'a transaction by which management of a business acquires a substantial stake in, and frequently effective control of, the business which it formerly managed, usually by means of financial arrangements tailored to suit individuals of relatively modest means'. In theory it is all very straightforward. The managers of a company take over a portion of the ownership of the company, while other external investors take over the rest. In practice, there are all kinds of buyouts, depending upon the circumstances of the company in question. Some of the commonest forms are:

- Where the management acquires all the ordinary shares. This usually occurs when the company is relatively small and does not have a great deal of assets. The cash to buy out the owners will be supplied as a loan, with a clearly defined schedule of repayment, or as redeemable preference shares (i.e. the holders of the ordinary shares can buy these shares back out of profits, but if the company should fail or be voluntarily wound up beforehand, the preference share holders have first rights on all the assets).
- Where the management holds a majority of the ordinary shares. Sometimes the investors will take ordinary shares themselves, if only to demonstrate to banks providing loan funds that they have faith in the company. Because the investors' equity share tends to reflect the price paid for the company versus the amount put up by the managers, such deals are also usually relatively small.
- Where the management holds only a minority of the ordinary shares. In general, the bigger the deal, the smaller the management shareholding. Where the institutions hold the majority of the shares, there also tends to be a heavy loan arrangement, mainly on non-equity liabilities such as loans and extended credit arrange-

ments. This kind of buyout, referred to as 'leveraged', can place a heavy strain on the company to maximize profits in the short term. Both the managers and the investors are gambling that sufficient profits will be created to pay off the loan. When it works, both the managers and the investors end up very wealthy. When it doesn't work, the company may be driven to its knees by a mountain of increasing debt.

By and large, British leveraged buyouts tend to be relatively conservative in their gearing, compared to similar US deals. Typically in the UK, the debt may be between 2.5 and five times the total equity, versus anything up to nine times in the United States.

In the latter kinds of buyout, the investment institution will normally look to see part of its return from dividends and part from floating the company on the Stock Exchange, the Unlisted Securities Market or the new Third Market – i.e. it will expect the value of the ordinary shares it owns to appreciate rapidly. Another popular form of exit route is by selling the company to another large organization. Whatever the chosen exit route, the institutions are putting increased pressure on the buyout managers to make it available quickly. While most buyouts are given three to five years, a considerable proportion are now brought to market at around 18 months – a very short time for a management team to make significant changes. This has led to comment that the managers are almost redundant in some buyouts; that the whole process is controlled and managed by the institutions, while the managers simply keep the business together.

The boom in buyouts has been fuelled by four things:

(i) Increasing awareness by managers that it is possible. Says one: 'Ten years ago, it would never have occurred to us to suggest a buyout. But when the occasion arose, a buyout seemed the obvious thing to do.' The awareness that buyouts are possible stems partly from well publicized examples and partly from the fact that accountants and other financial advisers now automatically consider buyouts as one of the options for companies in certain circumstances. Before 1981, however, financial advisers would not normally have given much thought to the buyout option because there were too many tax and regulatory obstacles, mainly centring around a key section in the Companies Act

1929. Section 54 was originally introduced to prevent someone acquiring a company through the use of its own assets and with virtually no capital of his or her own. Without this regulation, more or less anyone could arrange a temporary loan to purchase control of the company and then strip the business of its assets to repay the loan.

The effect of the regulation in the long-term was to inhibit banks and make them excessively wary of any deals which involved loan arrangements to managers and which might contravene the wide-ranging section 54. Only a few exceptional institutions dared to brave the legal complexities and managed to structure management buyouts which did not fall foul of legal restrictions. Most of the obstructions against buyouts were swept away by the Companies Act 1981 which, although it contained similar restrictions, granted important relaxations for private companies.

(ii) Increasing willingness by investors to support buyouts. From initial suspicion, City investors have come to like the management buyout because it offers a more stable investment than an unproven business start-up. Particularly where the company is a subsidiary of a large group, there is a strong argument for assuming that, given their head and a personal stake, the managers could make it much more profitable than it is at present. In many cases, simply removing the company from the overhead structure of its parent can make a radical improvement to profitability. Roger Brooke of Candover Investments maintains that there is typically a 5 per cent improvement in all-round performance when managers turn into owners.

(iii) Increasing willingness on the part of large companies to spin off elements that do not fit within the core of their businesses, or 'Cinderella subsidiaries'. Top management simply does not have the time to focus on disparate minor businesses at the expense of major, core businesses. These can be whole divisions, individual operating companies, or even small departments. During the 1960s and 1970s, there was a major acquisition boom. Gradually, companies have shaken out those businesses that do not fit within their central focus of activities. The process continues as companies attempt to become leaner and meaner in order to deter would-be predators in the current wave of acquisitions. Where acquisitions succeed, the first action taken by the new owners is frequently to sell off those parts of the company that do not fit the basic strategy. In all these circumstances, a buyout becomes one of the options top management may consider. About 80 per cent of buyouts are reported to arise from this cause.

Typical examples of large companies following this trend are Unilever and Sears Holdings. When Sears took over menswear chain Foster Brothers in 1985, it quickly sold off to the managers Jessops Tailor and Brownhills Clothing, as it did not want to retain this kind of manufacturing capability. It then sold two US retail subsidiaries to the managers for a further £6 million. Unilever found itself in the timber business as a result of acquiring Brooke Bond. It clearly did not fit the corporate profile, so timber company Mallinson-Denny was sold off to the managers for £90 million.

(An interesting sidelight on this kind of divestment is the manner in which many US companies have disposed of embarrassing subsidiaries in South Africa. The scarcity of management talent gives managers in that country a special edge when their company is to be sold, and there are examples of managers forcing the parent company to agree a buyout by threatening to quit if the company is sold to a competitor. Most of the buyout deals made by US and European companies with their South African subsidiaries involve an agreement on continuation of supplies and on the possibility of repurchase in the event of more stable political conditions. South African senior managers are reported to be particularly keen to undertake buyouts because their operations have been starved of investment as the parent companies are reluctant to expand there.)

(iv) Increasing privatization. Among the keenest supporters of buyouts have been the Conservative governments under Mrs Thatcher. Buyouts conform closely to the Conservatives' political goal of wider share ownership, particularly when they involve large numbers of employees rather than just the top layer of managers. Some of the largest buyouts, such as National Freight and Vickers Shipbuilding and Engineering, have been state sell-offs to employees, and at the time of writing other major state-owned industries are slated for similar treatment. The £200 million privatization of National Bus as local companies has seen a number of management buyouts, with buyout plans having been prepared for around 75 per cent of the 52 new companies. Leyland Bus was sold by the state-owned Rover Group to its managers. The Department of Energy, for example, has put a priority on moving the coal industry into the private sector. It considers that a sale to the employees as a whole, rather than just to management, would generate less vehement opposition from the trade unions. The plan, as revealed in *The Times*, is to divide up British Coal's 110 mines into eight areas, each of which would become an autonomous production company, with marketing handled by a central organization along the lines of the Milk Marketing Board. But the scheme depends upon a return to profitability; City investors are unlikely to support ventures that cannot show a significant profit potential.

For all three parties, however – vendor, investor and the managers – there are cons as well as pros in a buyout.

For the vendor company, a buyout saves hawking the company around – a harrowing process in which morale is likely to plummet, the best managers and professional employees are likely to start job hunting, and competitors get a chance to take a close and dangerous look into the operation. There are no fees to company brokers for arranging a sale and there is a greater prospect, if required, of maintaining an amicable relationship with the company for the supply of essential components or services. The disadvantage for the vendor is that the price is settled between accountants. Unless the vendor pits two sets of managers against each other, he may not receive the same terms as might be available from competitive bidding by several interested external parties.

For the investment institution, buyouts are one of the least risky investment options. 3i estimates that the failure rate is only about 14 per cent for small buyouts (less than £150,000) and only 4 per cent for larger ones. That makes for competition to participate in good buyouts, giving the managers a relatively strong hand in negotiations.

For the manager, there is an opportunity to get rich quick. It is widely reported that managers and employees of National Freight, who bought their company for £53.5 million in 1982, saw the value of their investment rise 2,700 per cent in four years. Similarly, managers at Stone International saw an exceptional return on the £250,000 they put up to buy their energy and electrical equipment group from the receiver in 1982. When the company was floated two years later, their 25 per cent shareholding became worth £7.5 million. There are probably hundreds of buyout millionaires in Britain already and many more who could be if they took their companies to market. According to *The Financial Times* 'One venture capital company alone, CIN Industrial Investments, the unquoted equity arm of the National Coal Board, claims to have created 40 millionaires through 23 of the 47 buyouts it has funded'. Few of these managers would have taken the risk of setting up their own business, even if they had had the capital to do so. Building on a business they know, with a team they know, is a much safer way of creating personal wealth.

Money, however, is not necessarily the major motivator. Equally, if not more, important is the challenge of really taking charge. Often, the managers will have been frustrated by the restrictions of being within a large group. They talk of being prevented from making investment decisions they considered essential, of the burdens of a huge central bureaucracy (one Canadian buyout company changed its fortunes for the better simply because it was no longer subject to the vagaries of the group computer system), and of being tied by conflicts of interest with other parts of the company. The following comments by managers who bought their firms out in the late 1970s are still typical:

- 'I don't have to justify my decisions to someone upstairs. We just have a quick, rational debate' – Walter Gibbon, chief executive of Radenton Ltd, a former subsidiary of BL.
- 'The politics has been taken out of our decision-making. We have been able to make a lot of changes in our products, which will have long-term benefits. Before, the group looked only for immediate growth in sales and bottom line figures' – Kenneth Hewitt, managing director of Thatchcode Ltd, an office filing manufacturer.
- 'Our company was very centralized. It imposed a great burden of reporting on us. Many people here were spending more time on

reporting than on running the business. It's a big relief to get out from under them.'

But no one claims it is easy. It requires very long hours and personal sacrifice. Tough decisions have to be made, not least about who should go and who should stay.

The risks are high in the early stages. Consider this true case: An engineering company decided to sell off a subsidiary in south London. The managers, led by the managing director and finance director, took the initiative and suggested that they should form a buyout consortium. The parent company dithered, forced them to make an offer, and used it to squeeze up the price offered by a competitor. When the competitor agreed to the increased price, the lead managers were sacked. In other cases, managers have been sacked on the spot, simply for suggesting a buyout, because the parent company management views it as an expression of disloyalty.

Other risks for the managers include losing their investment if the company should fail. For buyouts *do* fail. Hornby Hobbies, one of the case studies in this book, fell into spectacular losses a year after it was bought out. Women's underwear company Berlei was dragged under by its gearing; even with several rounds of refinancing, it eventually went into receivership and was taken over by Courtaulds. Linguaphone, too, had to be rescued within a year of being bought out from Westinghouse. Vosper Shiprepairers, taken over by its managers in 1985 from British Shipbuilders, called in accountants to administer the company under the Insolvency Act in February 1987, when it could not repay debts of £4.5 million. If the company does go into receivership, other creditors will usually have a prior call on the assets. Some buyout managers, who have given their homes as security for their stake in the company, have ended up without a roof over their heads.

Other buyout failures occur at the starting gate. Printing group McCorquodale attempted to use a buyout to prevent its rival Norton Opax gaining control in an unfriendly bid. But it was unable to convince the minority shareholders to sell. Anything less than 90 per cent acceptance would have prevented the company going private – in which case it would have had the impossible task of repaying a massive

£150 million of debt out of dividends. In the event, it failed to maintain its independence.

The managers of tobacco manufacturers Molins also fell foul of shareholders' rights when they attempted to buy out the company in a £50 million bid. Concerned at who would pick up the 29.9 per cent stake in the company that BAT Industries was determined to dispose of, the managers put in their own bid for the company as a whole. Even though they were supported by BAT, they were unable to convince the institutional shareholders that they were offering an adequate price.

Nonetheless, the ratio of the rewards to the risks is sufficiently high to make a buyout attractive to a good proportion of managers. There is also emerging a kind of machismo that makes the manager, who fails to seize the buyout opportunity when it is offered, seem weak and indecisive. The buyout phenomenon is clearly here to stay.

In the following chapters we shall examine in practical terms, for both managers and vendors, how to go about deciding when the opportunity is ripe for a buyout, how to approach it and how to carry it through. We then illustrate the lessons through case studies of companies that have gone through buyouts, with differing levels of success. Finally, in the appendices, we review a survey of 54 boughtout companies, which we conducted in the Spring of 1987. Our questionnaire looked at the circumstances of the buyout, experiences with advisers and backers, the terms of the deal and post buyout performance. It throws much light on the problems managers encounter, from the point of the initial offer through to the running of the new business. We also provide a list of useful contacts and sources of information for those managers who are just starting, or about to start, down the buyout trail. We wish them luck.

Table 1 *Analysis of 1986/87 management buyouts by quarter*

Quarter	*MBOs over £10m.* Number	Value £m.	*Estimated value of smaller MBOs* £m.	*Total Value* £m.
1986				
I	10	320	70	390
II	7	210	70	280
III	6	180	70	250
IV	6	170	60	230
	29	880	270	1,150
1987				
I	3	190	60	250

Source: *Peat Marwick McLintock, 1 April 1987*

Table 2 *Estimate of total UK management buyouts*

	Number	Value £m
1980	100	40
1981	170	120
1982	190	230
1983	200	230
1984	190	260
1985	230	1,020
1986	270	1,150
	1,350	3,050
Annual average	190	440

Source: *Peat Marwick McLintock, 1 April 1987*

Table 3 *Larger management buyouts 1981/87 by size*
(Total Funding in £m.)

£m.	1981	1982	1983	1984	1985	1986	1987 (to date)
10 – 25	4	4	4	4	12	18	1
25 – 50		1	3	2		5	
50 – 75		1		1	3	3	1
75 – 100					2	2	
100+					1	1	1
Total	4	6	7	7	18	29	3

Source: *Peat Marwick McLintock, 1 April 1987*

Table 4 *Larger management buyouts 1981/87 (total funding in £m.)*

£m.	1981	1982	1983	1984	1985	1986	1987 (to date)
Under 25	Famous Names (8) Hornby (10) Gleneagles (13) Ansafone (14)	Isis (8) Stanley Gibbons (9) Stone (18) Amalgamated Foods (21)	SPP Group (9) E & Am Ins (10) Thermalite (12) Victaulic (15)	Evans Halshaw (9) Westbury (12) DRI (22) Paragon (24)	Brymon Airways (9) Bison (10) Willis Faber (10) Tibbet & Britten (10) MENCC (12) Record Ridgway (13) Secure Homes (13) Royco (13) Vosper Thornycroft (19) Ellerman Lines (19) Wades (19) Bradstock Group Ins (20)	Trend Communications (10) Exacta (10) Partco (10) Leyland Bus (10) KDG Instruments (11) Jeyes Hygiene (11) Maccess (11) Furmanite (12) Gomme (12) European Industrial Services (12) Intercraft Designs (15) Cundell Corrugated (15) Nestor BNA (15) Computing Devices (19) HUS Deposits (19) Haleworth (20) Technitron (21) Berkertex (22)	Holliday Dyes (12)
25 – 50		First Leisure (44)	Hugin (26) Timpson (42) Collier (47)	Wordplex (28) Simplex (29)		AMF Legg (25) Evans Healthcare (27) Bowater Paper (38) City Merchant Developers (40) Norwest Holst (45)	
50 – 75		NFC (53)		Target (50)	St. Regis (52) Manugood (60) Caradon (61)	Unipart (52) TIP Europe (60) Parker Pen (74)	Fairey (51)
75 – 100					Mallinson-Denny (93) Mecca Leisure (95)	British United Shoe Machinery (80) Premier Brands (97)	
100+					Lawson Mardon (280)	Vickers Shipbuilders (100)	Wickes (124)

Source: *Peat Marwick McLintock, 1 April 1987*

PMM have acted for the purchasers in 33/74 of the above cases involving total funds of over £1.1bn.
Larger management buyouts are taken as those with total funding of over £10m. in 1986 values.

1

How to Begin a Buyout

'The first phase is a sifting out process when many buyout teams inevitably fall by the wayside' – Steven Bruck, Pannell Kerr Forster, international accountants.

In many ways, the most difficult and stressful phase of a buyout is when it is still in its embryonic form. Acting on incomplete information, the aspiring manager strongly believes that a buyout is feasible. Knowing who it is safe to talk to is a major dilemma; it is always possible that the owners will react in a hostile way to the idea of a buyout. If so, the manager may find himself regarded as a traitor in the camp and be dismissed, or simply not be trusted, with no possibility of further career progression. The potential damage to the manager's career in a company cannot be overestimated. On the other hand, the potential rewards are also high. It is this balance of risk and reward which fascinates so many entrepreneurial managers. Yet the manager's dreams of staging a buyout often never become more than just a dream.

The intricate nature of the buyout process does not make it any easier. While many managers will be familiar with the basic concept, dealing with the reality is a different thing altogether. When and how should the manager declare his interest to the vendor, for instance? When should external advisers and financiers enter the scene? At what point should the manager assemble a management team? Whatever he decides to do, the manager will have to start talks almost immediately with three different groups: potential members of the management team, financial advisers and, at a slightly later stage, the vendor itself.

Much time can be saved and some early mistakes avoided if a manager has a clear notion of the different stages of a buyout. Inevitably, some of these phases will overlap, while others will be considerably more complex and drawn out. The process can be broken into five distinct phases, each of which will have its own complications and problems.

Stage 1 – The idea:

- considering a buyout
- forming a management team
- contacting a professional adviser
- determining whether the company is for sale.

Stage 2 – Preparing the proposal:

- conducting a feasibility study
- approaching potential financiers
- agreeing a broad price range with the vendor

Stage 3 – Obtaining finance:

- targeting specific financiers and presenting them with a detailed proposal
- obtaining an agreement, in principle, to provide finance.

Stage 4 – Negotiating the deal:

- negotiating with the vendor
- agreeing terms
- structuring the deal

In this chapter we shall look at the groundwork that must be covered in Stage 1.

Considering a Buyout

Buyouts can involve companies of almost every size, and in any business sector, ranging from the £273 million deal for Mardon Packaging, the £10 million deal for Hornby toy manufacturers, through to a small local deal involving only a few hundred thousand pounds.

They can involve near bankrupt companies, profitable subsidiaries, or risk-averse mature businesses.

Broadly speaking, it is possible to identify several situations where a company or division is ripe for investment. Possible candidates include:

- Family-run businesses where the owner has died or is retiring, or where the family is no longer involved in day-to-day management. Selling to the company's management is often an effective way of solving succession problems and ensures that the transfer of ownership happens smoothly. Suppliers and customers are reassured by the business's continuing stability and by the fact that it has passed into familiar hands.
- An independent business about to go into receivership. In this case, a buyout is often the last resort for the management team. The receiver often favours a buyout because it avoids costs such as redundancy payments, dilapidation costs on leases and other liabilities. Selling the entire business to the team is also a better overall realization of its value than selling the assets piecemeal.
- A parent company going into receivership, which has a number of viable subsidiaries or divisions. These operations may be bought out by several management teams, while the parent company is liquidated.
- All or part of the operations of a nationalized company in the process of being privatized. Under the present government, public sector buyouts are increasingly common and include National Freight, Land Rover from British Leyland and Vickers Shipbuilding and Engineering (VSEL). Partly for political reasons of encouraging wider share ownership, these deals often involve employee share schemes. When Vickers acquired Cammell Laird and its building yards at Birkenhead and Barrow-in-Furness for instance, the company instantly issued a glossy 100–page prospectus, inviting Cammell's 8,000 employees, plus company pensioners and citizens of the two towns, to participate and help finance the buyout.

A large number of opportunities for buyouts exist in new transition conglomerates undergoing restructure.

Most large companies go through cycles of acquisition and diversification, and cycles of disposal and concentration. During the concentration cycle, units which do not fit into the core operations of the business are either closed or sold, depending on profitability and the availability of an acceptable buyer. This kind of rationalization often occurs shortly after the appointment of a new chief executive, eager to make his mark. One of the easiest ways for him to do this is to restructure the organization. To identify this kind of opportunity, the buyout manager must be closely aware of top management attitudes and objectives. If his unit is targeted as a major 'star' within the corporate strategy, his proposal is less likely to be welcomed than if it is regarded as 'obscure'.

In a very few cases, management buyouts have been used as a defence against predatory bids for a quoted company by third parties. Later we shall examine the case of Haden, a major buyout which was made under these circumstances. There are two main difficulties with this type of buyout:

(i) it is still sufficiently novel for financial institutions to be wary;

(ii) there is not just one vendor to negotiate with but perhaps many thousands, as the buyout team must obtain agreement to sell from the vast majority of shareholders.

Other likely opportunities for buyouts include:

- assets or plants, sold off when the vendor wishes to reduce borrowings or to release capital for more important projects
- product lines failing to fulfil their profit potential
- sales resulting from a rationalization programme
- a subsidiary which lacks the commitment of the parent company and loses out in terms of funding and support
- a subsidiary which is geographically distant. In cases which involve production operations, a company with excess capacity may decide to sell a distant unit and strengthen production nearer its home base
- peripheral operations, sold off because they do not fit into the parent's portfolio, or because the company is moving into new areas of business. Although a subsidiary may be highly profitable,

it no longer has any strategic value or interest for the parent company.

- loss-making or marginally profitable operating units.

This last type of buyout certainly seems to be increasingly common. The volatile market conditions and the acquisition fever which has gripped the City of London in the last couple of years has led to companies becoming almost neurotic about the stability of their share prices. The buyout at International Leisure Group in the Spring of 1987, for example, was largely due to the group's concern over 'the volatile and intensely competitive market conditions affecting ILG's traditional tour operating business which have sometimes impacted unfavourably on the group's reported results in recent years'. Some analysts also believed the buyout was due to fears that a new damaging war in overseas holidays was about to begin.

The trend towards selling off peripheral businesses is a major reason for the increasing number of buyouts in Britain. Roger Brooke, of Candover Investments, explained to *The Sunday Times:* 'Increasing numbers of parent companies have been looking at their companies and have been more willing to make divestments than ever before.' This attitude is fuelled in part by the growing practice of North American companies of shedding their European activities. Gelco, for example, the US leasing and transport company, sold its European trailer operations in 1986 to managers for £60 million. Although Gelco gave no reason for the sale of TIP-Europe, it is widely thought that the company wanted to concentrate on its US activities, particularly on CTI, the world's largest container leasing company.

'We expect a substantial number of such deals from this direction', said Brooke. 'As American companies prune their portfolios, especially after the recent mega-mergers, they often look at the distant ones.'

Many British companies are also in the process of concentrating on mainstream activities. Mecca Leisure, for example, was bought out in 1985 from Grand Metropolitan, the hotels and gambling conglomerate. Grandmet made it clear that it wanted only Mecca's betting shop and casino interests. Its other concerns – the bingo halls, ballrooms and holiday camps – had no place in the conglomerate's portfolio.

With so many opportunities around, managers are biding their time and waiting for the right political and financial moment to approach the vendor. Timing is of crucial importance. Cadbury-Schweppes, for instance, would probably have dismissed Tony Wardell's idea of buying the group's aerosol subsidiary in 1981. As it was, Wardell waited some four more years until he felt his position was strong enough for the company to react positively to the notion. His suggestion for a buyout in 1985 was greeted with open arms by Cadbury-Schweppes.

Wardell first thought of doing a buyout when he began to doubt the group's commitment to the future of Aerosols International. The subsidiary was performing badly, its export market was rapidly disappearing, and it appeared as though Cadbury-Schweppes saw the aerosols business as no longer fitting into its corporate identity. At that time, Wardell was a commercial manager. He had discussed the possibility of a buyout with the National Westminster Bank, but had postponed it because he felt he did not have enough weight with Cadbury-Schweppes and the subsidiary's management team. He also believed that Aerosol's poor performance would deter managers from undertaking a buyout as the investment would seem too risky.

Circumstances began to look more rosy when Wardell was appointed general manager of Aerosols International at the beginning of 1984. He moved the subsidiary into areas of the market which would give better margins, and where fewer rivals were present and opportunities for new business existed. After two years, the company was in profit and had been showing higher returns on capital employed than practically any other subsidiary in the group. It was now clear that Cadbury-Schweppes was disenchanted with the aerosol business and that financial problems in other areas were causing the group to seek ways of withdrawing from the health and hygiene business.

Ironically, the danger now was that Wardell's offer to buy out the subsidiary would come too late. 'There was a chance of the baby going down the plughole with the bathwater', he explained to *Business World*. Rather than wait around for the group to sell off the subsidiary, Wardell made what he called a 'pre-emptive strike' by making an offer for the business. In February 1986, the deal for £3.4 million was agreed, with Wardell taking 27 per cent of the shares.

Although in most cases the initial notion will come from one or several members of the buyout team, suggestions can sometimes come from the parent company itself. In cases of a bankrupt company, the receiver will often suggest a buyout; in nationalized companies, the idea nearly always comes from the vendor.

The manner in which the parent company initiates the buyout will depend on its sensitivity and political overtones. If the buyout will save jobs in an ailing company or division, for example, it will probably suit the parent company to broadcast the buyout openly and invite managers to a broad discussion. If the vendor feels that the sale will cast an unfavourable light on its overall performance and attract unwanted media attention, it will probably prefer to make a discreet hint, perhaps through an informal talk or over drinks. One successful buyout, for example, arose from what seemed ostensibly a joke. A financier describes how one of his clients came to initiate a buyout: 'After discussions during a group board meeting about selling off his division, one of the other directors approached him, clapped him on the back and said "So you'll be thinking of a buyout, I expect".'

'Buyouts are increasingly being engineered by the parent companies themselves, but now managers are having greatness thrust upon them,' says Robert Smith of Charterhouse Development Capital. 'In some sectors, buyouts are becoming standard practice. It used to be that managers would meet secretly in the pub, almost wearing balaclavas. Now, the moment a parent company announces that an operation or subsidiary is up for sale, a buyout team is in its office first thing the next morning.'

A company selling consumer goods used a buyout to get rid of a senior executive who plainly wanted a quiet life and more time to play golf. The company approached him and asked if he would like to buy out the unit under his control. It pointed him towards financial advice and hoped he would take the bait. The manager did. Using this tactic, the group got rid of a peripheral unit and an unwanted executive.

Negotiations are significantly easier if a buyout has been solicited by the vendor, although the management team will probably need to work harder to convince financiers of their commitment. If you are ever in this situation, be prepared to be asked why you waited to be invited to do a buyout. You may also be asked whether your failure initially to recognize the opportunity indicated a lack of entrepreneurial ability. If the vendor seems too enthusiastic about the buyout, financiers may suspect a catch; is it trying to land the management team with a lame duck?

Forming a Management Team

> 'In the end, you are backing the man, and after 11 years with 3i that, more than anything else, is burnt on my heart. Although balance sheets and products are important, those could be off and you would still back the man.' – John Kingston, director of Investors in Industry (3i), Bristol.

While you can assess the suitability of a buyout by means of hard-nosed financial analysis, picking a management team will ultimately depend on instinct and luck. The task will be one of the most crucial and difficult that a manager will face throughout the buyout. Negotiations will come to a swift end if any of the management team appear weak or incompetent, while shaking off an unwanted team member before completion of the buyout is a messy and often acrimonious task.

Before negotiations begin, the buyout leader will have the unenviable job of weighing up dispassionately colleagues and friends, some of whom he or she may have worked with for years. If the appropriate candidates are not obviously to hand, it may be wiser for the buyout leader to approach an adviser immediately to obtain help on selection. If certain crucial skills are glaringly lacking in the pool of talent available, the adviser may help the buyout leader to recruit managers outside the organization. If difficulties with the team are likely to arise, an early approach to an adviser should ensure that problems are ironed out before they become a major stumbling-block.

When selecting a team, the buyout leader must be aware of the strengths and weaknesses of potential team members, be able to judge how they will work together and, a still harder task, assess whether they can make the transition from working in the relatively secure corporate environment to running an independent company. Although the company and the product or service that it is offering will still be the same, the new management team will have a huge change in responsibilities, powers, functions and reporting relations. They will undoubtedly be exposed to new pressures and strains.

'The conversion of a corporate mentality to the entrepreneurial activity is a major source of difficulty and the biggest trauma the buyout team will face', asserts Neil Falkner, chairman of Development Capital Group. 'It can take a couple of years before the whole team has adjusted to owning and running a business.'

Qualities your team will need are:

(i) Commitment to the business

If a management team is anything less than 100 per cent committed to the buyout, it should seriously consider whether it should proceed. Negotiations will be gruelling and the amount of detailed research and preparation needed will almost certainly mean that the team will be burning the midnight oil. Attending to the buyout and continuing at the same time to run the business on a day-to-day basis is a formidable and exhausting job. Managers who attempt to do this with only half-hearted enthusiasm for the buyout are doomed to failure, inflicting great harm on themselves and the rest of the team. If a team member drops out halfway through negotiations it may damage the credibility of the lead manager who selected him, and throw a question mark over the team's fitness to buy the company.

There is also the problem of keeping the business solvent and profitable while spending management time on negotiation. And there is an additional dilemma; do you push up performance to gain the confidence of the financial institutions, or do you depress performance to lower the price, an unethical and risky second option. This last option, besides being unethical, could backfire on the team and lead to serious misgivings about their competency. It may be worth splitting the team into two, one half to handle the negotiations, the other half to run the company. This tactic could also give you an opportunity to grow any younger or more junior team members.

Advisers and financiers will undoubtedly be looking for total commitment from the team. Before they progress with negotiations, advisers need to believe that they have a group of individuals who are willing to work around the clock for the sake of the business – both before and after the buyout. They look for a team that believes it has something unique to bring to the business and that is totally dedicated to seeing the business succeed.

A desire to get rich quick is probably not, in itself, a strong enough reason for a buyout. A survey in 1986 by Sebastian Green, of the London Business School, clearly showed the importance of being committed first and foremost to the boughtout company. The survey, *The Meaning of Ownership in Management Buyouts*, was based on detailed interviews with 43 executives in ten buyouts, which were mainly divested subsidiaries of larger companies or sales from receivership. These executives believed that commitment to the business was a far more important motive than that of financial reward. One executive commented: 'Either you're committed to the business or you're not, and having an ownership stake in it won't affect that. If you enjoy your job then you are giving everything of yourself, irrespective of whether you are working for yourself or for a corporation.'

Choosing team members who are over-concerned with the size of their equity stake in the business will inevitably lead to problems, especially when the equity terms are being drawn up. Management teams have been known to quarrel bitterly over their stake in the business, especially when a two-tier system of equity shares exists. In many buyouts, the buyout leader and perhaps two other key managers are given more equity shares than the rest of the team. An alternative arrangement is for the whole of the management team to hold most of the equity, with a small proportion reserved for personnel who are less critical to the well-being of the business.

Whatever the arrangement, some sort of differential will exist and can be a cause for resentment, especially if the individuals concerned have gone into the buyout with the mistaken assumption that they will become millionaires overnight. The 'greedometer factor', as it is sometimes called, can have a far-reaching and destructive impact and should not be underestimated. Awareness of this possibility when choosing the team can lessen the likelihood of it happening.

There is difficulty in including people who overestimate their own worth as a potential asset to the buyout team. Giving them an equity stake and a significant say in the running of the company can cause real problems after the buyout. The team leader should remember that deadbeats on the team can and do hinder progress. Although possible, it is much more difficult to get rid of people who hold shares than those who do not.

In summary, you must be absolutely sure that this person really is going to contribute a lot *now*, and that he will not be outgrown as the company progresses.

The key question is 'Are these the people who can take this company to the Unlisted Securities Market (USM) with me?'

What do you do about it, if not? Anyone excluded at this juncture will be resentful, but you cannot afford to take weak links with you. You must look for strong replacements who can take the company in the direction it needs to go.

(ii) A balanced and broad range of management skills

It is essential that management teams are well balanced and cover the whole range of management tasks, including sales, marketing, production and finance. Where technical or design skills crucially affect the company's ability to stay ahead in competitive and rapidly moving markets, it will probably be necessary to have these disciplines also represented on the management team.

Although statistically unproven, it is widely believed that a weak management team is one of the main reasons why buyouts fail. In some cases, the management team has failed to show that it is capable of operating independently from the vendor; in the case of sale by a receiver, managers have been unable to demonstrate that they have the ability to turn the business around. The receiver may also have concluded that the company's troubles were due to the poor management. Steven Bruck of Pannell Kerr Forster maintains: 'At the end of the day, inexperienced management is a killer and the most obvious reason for most buyouts failing.

A common weakness is that teams are skilled in a limited range of disciplines only and that they lack the strategic and managerial skills necessary for running a business. Such a limitation was true of the failed bid to buy out Richard Shops and John Collier from Hanson Trust. Although the group supported the idea of a management buyout and had already used the technique to divest at least one other subsidiary the deal still failed. At the end of the day, Hanson Trust decided that the composition of the management team was not adequate, especially in the buying function, an area of the retail industry which the group considered essential.

Particular concern should be given to choosing the finance director of the new management team. This role is crucial when the team begins negotiating with the financial institutions. The financial director will be best able to supply the detailed information about the company's past history and financial performance which the institutions will call for. Grave doubts will be expressed if the management team cannot obtain this type of detail or if it seems out of its depth with the kind of financial information required.

The buyout leader should ensure that his financial director is capable of taking on far more complex duties and responsibilities. The director will, in effect, become company secretary and will have to deal with company auditors and shareholders. He or she may have to deal with problems arising from poor performance, or from rapid growth. According to a number of buyout investment funds, finance directors of buyouts often find themselves out of their depth and have to be replaced at a very early stage.

In the short term during the buyout itself, financial advisers can be a stop-gap, at least making sure that the business plan is credible and has the information the institutions need, in the manner they prefer. At the same time, they can often direct the buyout team to suitable non-executive directors, who can add clout and experience to the negotiations. This principle applies to all areas of management weakness. On the marketing side for example, the Institute of Marketing retains a register of recommended consultants, many of whom have relevant experience. More generally, both the Bank of England and the Institute of Directors maintain services that match-make between companies and experienced individuals for non-executive positions.

(iii) Entrepreneurial skills

Few management teams go very far down the road in a buyout before they discover that every major party they deal with wants to be sure that they have sufficient entrepreneurial skill to run the new business. The management team must be able to see the business in its broadest perspective, understand the company as one functioning whole and be capable of taking important strategic decisions about the future of the company.

Vendor, advisers, financiers and shareholders will be under no illusions about the difficulty of the task facing the management team. No longer under the protective umbrella of the parent company, the team may have to acquire many new skills very quickly. It will have to begin servicing a much higher level of debt and cope with the cashflow implications that debt brings with it. Suppliers and customers will need to be reassured about the stability of the business; the workforce may be concerned about any changes to its work agreements. Certainly, the management team will have to display a determination, resourcefulness and adaptability probably rarely called for in their former positions.

What are the chances that the buyout leader will be able to find entrepreneurial managers? The classic image of the entrepreneur is of a dynamic, innovative, impatient individual who, like a fish out of water, cannot survive in the alien corporate environment. Constantly fighting against bureaucratic restraints and controls, the budding entrepreneur is a thorn in the organization's flesh until he or she finally leaves to set up an independent business.

If that was truly the case, entrepreneurial ability would be a scarce, almost extinct, commodity in the majority of businesses, and most, if not all, management buyout teams would have either abandoned their hopes, taken up fishing and worked for early retirement or else quit to start their own business long before. It is increasingly recognized, however, that most of today's businesses contain hidden entrepreneurs or 'intrapreneurs'. These individuals have latent entrepreneurial skills that can be kindled into full strength with the right sort of incentive. A buyout, with its promise of freedom, independence, challenge and wider responsibilities and power, can flush out such people.

Some entrepreneurial individuals will be easy to spot; they will often have a high profile in the company, be notorious for wanting to rush ahead with new projects, and constantly challenge accepted traditions and procedures. They will have plenty of energy and enthusiasm, with a tendency to think up grandiose schemes and ignore detail.

Latent entrepreneurs are harder to spot, but some identifiable traits include:

- strong motivation to achieve and to climb the corporate rungs as high as possible
- keen desire for independence and belief that he or she can run the business or operation better

- dislike of repetitive, routine tasks
- commitment to his or her job and to the organization
- entrepreneurial relatives, spouses or friends
- activity in community affairs or local politics
- insistence on knowing the results of decisions that affect his or her area of responsibility
- willingness to take risks (but preference for a moderate risk rather than either a high risk with an outside chance of high return or a slight risk with little challenge).

Don't be tempted into thinking that the buyout will force your team to develop entrepreneurial qualities. If anything, the buyout will discourage innovation and risk-taking, so the team needs to be particularly strong in this area to counter those pressures.

For instance, a key discovery in Green's survey mentioned previously, was that buyout teams are often forced by circumstances to adopt a conservative approach to many aspects of business after the buyout. Because of the high gearing of the business, they implement short-run cashflow management. Because investment in new processes or products has cashflow implications, the company finds itself adopting only those investments that have minimal risk and short-term payback. It will almost always be encouraged in these attitudes by the institutional investors. While a strongly entrepreneurial team will probably thrive under these difficulties, a more staid team may find its entrepreneurial capabilities seriously sapped and it may take several years before it feels sufficiently sure of itself (i.e. when its gearing is reduced to more moderate proportions) to spread its wings and fly.

Another common misconception is that the prospect of financial gain will cause entrepreneurial skills to surface in managers. Research into entrepreneurship has revealed that the money motive is of only relatively minor importance compared to the desire for independence and the excitement of the entrepreneur's vision of what can be achieved. This should be just as true for the management team.

In Green's survey, the managers' equity stake from the buyout did not, in itself, encourage them to be more entrepreneurial. Many of the executives in his survey did not even have a full sense of ownership because of their awareness of the external equity involvement. One of the executives commented:

> This is not like owning 100 per cent of the business. You have to be careful because you are dealing with other people's money. I suppose my philosophy is that I take greater risks with my own money than with other people's.

(iv) Ability to withstand pressure and adapt to change

Because of the high stakes and the ever present possibility of negotiations breaking down, buyouts can be difficult and exhausting experiences. The team will sometimes be under tremendous tension, particularly if the vendor is uncooperative or even hostile and has not granted the team sufficient time to prepare its proposal. The strain and attrition on the management team can become even more severe if a competitor makes a counter bid for the company or division.

All in all, the team will be facing challenges that they have never had to face before. As Robert Smith of Charterhouse Development Capital explains:

> They are virtually undergoing a change of life. Up to that point, they have been corporate animals who have learned their way up by observing rules and filling in forms. A buyout suddenly entails real financial risk and real exposure. Some team members do crack eventually. All through negotiations the team is hyped up. It often feels both scared and elated. The stakes are *total* for these people; it's a big moment in each manager's life and means far more than promotion. Under this strain, it's inevitable that there will be casualties, both before and after the buyout.

The battle to survive these pressures does not end even after the deal is signed. The management team will have little time to relax. Indeed, some say that this is the time the hard work really starts. It must instantly establish its credibility with its suppliers, customers and workforce, and shift the business into top gear.

When selecting the team, the buyout leader should take every opportunity to observe how his or her colleagues work under pressure and in times of crisis. Once a manager has been invited onto the team, the tremendous pressures that he or she is likely to experience for a number of months or even years should be spelt out clearly.

(v) Team cohesiveness

If the buyout is to succeed, the management team must think and act together as a cohesive whole. In many ways, negotiating the buyout will be like a speeded-up version of running the company. Under intense pressure, the team will have to take key strategic and financial decisions. In a short period of months, it must display a unity and strength which most executive teams take years to develop.

Mutual trust and respect are also important elements in the buyout team. Each manager is taking a substantial risk and putting his or her own money on the line. Each manager must know that the other team members are dependable and trustworthy. This team unity will certainly be either damaged or stunted if any member of the team is motivated solely by self-interest.

One manager who was involved in a successful buyout two years ago describes how the experience made a fundamental impact upon him: 'In my former position, I saw myself in terms of someone leading others and rarely as a team member. The buyout totally changed my outlook. Now I see myself as a member of a team.'

A strong commitment to the business and to each other ensures that the team will not degenerate into a squabbling group of individuals. As one manager commented in Green's survey:

> There are differences of opinion about priorities and the like, but there seems to be a tacit agreement that the reason we are arguing strongly is that we all want the same thing. We want the company to be profitable. Now we are talking in a common framework and not criticising anyone.

(vi) Strong leadership

Research has shown that some management teams fall into the mistake of management by committee. It is normally safe to assume that most of the team members have demonstrated independent and forceful personalities by their very willingness to risk their jobs and join the buyout. If they are committed to the buyout, they will have strong views about how the negotiations should proceed and the way the new company should be run. It is very easy for this situation to deteriorate until the team becomes split by in-fighting and severely hampered in its ability to make decisions. One individual *must* take the role of leader if the buyout is to succeed.

As each manager has an equity stake in the business, he has an equal entitlement to express his views. The buyout leader, therefore, will often lead the team only through force of character and genuine leadership qualities. With this in mind, the buyout team should avoid the use of seniority as a basis for selecting a leader. Equally, the team members should not automatically take their place in the hierarchy from their current organizational positions. If they do choose to do so, problems can arise later on when a younger, more junior manager begins to exhibit obvious leadership qualities. An out-and-out fight for the leadership may ensue, with the team split by dividing loyalties.

In some cases, such as that of Roadchef, an individual manager is so clearly the dynamic force behind the buyout that he assumes the majority of the equity himself. This has obvious advantages and disadvantages. One of the decisions he must make is what proportion of the equity to award to his colleagues.

The size of the buyout team

The buyout team has two dimensions. The first consists of the would-be shareholders. They may be either a handful of managers at the top (most buyouts are teams of three or five people), a wider segment of key managers (for example, thirty at Roadchef), or all willing employees as at National Freight.

Research has revealed that a very small proportion, some 8 per cent, involve only one person, while at the other extreme, the largest known management team has numbered around 42 people, 16 of them directors, in a buyout of an international company with 25 subsidiaries.

The decision about the number of internal shareholders rests on:

(i) Timing: the larger the shareholding, the more complex the arrangements. In a race against deadlines, the smaller the number of participants, the better.

(ii) Motivation: one of the benefits of a buyout is that it allows the company to lock in and 'incentivize' those people most critical to its success. By including some people and excluding others you are making clear statements about their perceived value to the organization.

The second dimension consists of the negotiating team. A large number of shareholders must delegate full power to them. This team should number at least two and no more than five people.

The broad rule is that the bigger the team, the greater the risk of failure. A large negotiating team increases the possibility that disagreements will set in or that someone will decide to drop out. It may be less effective and close-knit, with decisions generally taking longer to make. A smaller team decreases the chance that damaging leaks will occur during sensitive stages of the buyout.

But in some cases, a large negotiating team will be appropriate. In major conglomerates or in international companies, for instance, the number of key personnel may be quite large. The team can be expanded to include departmental heads if more involvement and support for the buyout need to be generated.

An unwise reason for increasing the size of the management is to raise extra funds to finance the buyout. Some managers argue that this is a way of avoiding the servicing costs of external funding. In reality, however, the higher the price, the greater the possibility that more than one financial institution will be involved. Another strong reason for a small team is the need for the management equity stake to remain significant. Research has shown that the smaller the team, the more likely it is to hold a majority equity stake. In general, financial institutions prefer to see a clearly identifiable management group. If equity holdings are shared out too widely, the institutions feel that the ownership incentive becomes too diluted.

Contacting a Professional Adviser

Sound independent advice, preferably right at the start of the buyout, is a *must* for the management team. Structuring the terms of the deal without professional help would be the same as wandering through a financial maze. The legal, tax and pension arrangements alone are far too tortuous for the team to handle unaided.

National Freight's chairman, Sir Peter Thompson, commented after the buyout: 'I had no concept of what we would have to do to satisfy the law – the prospectus went through 33 proofs before we finally got it right'. One manager is strongly critical of the professional help he received. The final salt in the wound was that 'despite extortionate fees, our advisers seemed to expect us to do all the work. We just got terribly frustrated and at a number of stages we said "forget it".'

If the team wants to get the best from its advisers, it should make sure they have extensive experience of management buyouts. If not, the team may find the advisers fail to obtain the best deal and take far too long to make decisions. Good advisers are often best found by relying on personal recommendations from people who have successfully achieved buyouts. As well as specialist management consultants, selected accountants and solicitors can provide essential business advice.

Allocation of Responsibility

General advisers – Use them as a sounding-board to help develop a negotiating strategy, set a price and formulate future business proposals. They can suggest further advisers and coordinate their efforts for you. Their other duty could be to find and negotiate sources of finance.

Accountants – Use them to investigate the accounts and financial affairs of the target company. They can negotiate financial terms and the price payable and advise on cashflow and taxation.

Solicitors – Once the terms of the deal have been agreed, their main responsibility is to carry it through to completion. They work out the detailed terms, prepare and amend contracts and advise on the tax implications of the new company structure.

The banks and financiers – They provide finance through loans or equity participation, and search for and arrange outside funding. When dealing with financial institutions, quotes should be invited from a number of firms in order to exert pressure for competitive terms.

Surveyors – They can value freehold property and long leasehold and advise on dilapidation liabilities.

Payment – In cases where the professional adviser is unwilling to quote a fee before the job is completed, even the roughest estimate he can give is a useful guide. If the team uses a specialist advisory group, it may be economic to negotiate contracts on a payment-by-results basis.

Organizational document

As the idea for the buyout becomes a reality, the arena becomes more crowded as new managers are invited on to the team, professional advisers are commissioned, and discussions with the vendor begin. Now is the time for the management team to draw up a detailed agenda to ensure that tasks are properly delegated and that everyone has the information they need.

Accountants Blackstone, Franks, Smith & Co. recommend the following checklist:

(i) *Objectives* – including a timetable of target achievements and how they will be fulfilled.

(ii) *Advisers* – the names and addresses of both your advisers and those of the vendor.

(iii) *Problem areas* – a list of the potential problems and the delegation of their solutions.

(iv) *Information* – if the buyout requires the purchasing of shares in a company, you need to note the company's name, company number and its place and date of incorporation. You need the details of its existing authorized and issue share capital, the names and addresses of its shareholders (specifying their holdings), the names and addresses of directors, and the name and address of the company auditors.

If the buyout involves buying underlying assets and businesses from a company, you need to list the name and address of the owner, the main assets of the company (even those which are not to be acquired), an outline of the target business, and details of the trading or other contracts concerning the business.

(v) *Information for advisers* – The solicitors and accountants require the following details about the target company:

– recent audited accounts

– recent reports on its activity

– articles of association and memorandum

– rules and trust deeds of any pension or life assurance scheme

– details of share options, share incentive or profit sharing schemes

– all outstanding loan stocks, charges and mortgages

– leases and tenancy agreements granted

– valuations and title deeds of freehold and leasehold property owned

– all loans and agreements of indebtedness

– all indemnities and guarantees

– any material litigation involving the target company.

Is the Company for Sale?

At some point, managers will have to take their courage in their hands and approach the vendor to see if the business is for sale. Time pressures will obviously determine the best moment of approach. If there is no immediate necessity to make a bid, they can carefully prepare their offer, formulate a line of attack about the advantages of a buyout for the vendor, and make initial contacts with potential backers. Unfortunately, many managers will not have this luxury, but will be racing against other competitors, or against the threat of closure or liquidation. In these circumstances, they will have to declare their interest to the vendor very early on, perhaps even before they have drawn up the entire management team, or contacted professional advisers.

In many buyouts, especially in the case of a company about to be liquidated, or where the owner is retiring, the team will already have firm information that the vendor will consider the sale. For the management team heading a subsidiary, and where the parent company has not publicly announced any plans for divestment, the initial approach will be fraught with difficulties. If the bid is likely to receive a hostile response, the team should think about trying to gain some allies at headquarters before it makes a formal offer. It should make sure that it can prove to the vendor that it has financial backing and that it can pay a competitive price for the target business.

If its offer is rejected, the team should not automatically give up. Alan Dennis' initial £2 million offer to buy out Wayne Kerr Render, a small electronics company, from the US Rockwell International, was rejected out of hand. Rockwell insisted on a price of £3 million for the subsidiary. After a string of possible buyers had looked over the company but declined to offer such a high price, the US group reluctantly accepted that its price was unrealistic. Nothing further happened for a year.

Dennis, who headed WKR's electronic interests, told *Management Today:*

> Rockwell, the directors and all the employees all knew what was going on, and the problem was to hold the company together. It would have folded up in another six months – I lost my technical director to the headhunters and some others down the line resigned.

Rockwell finally ground into action and accepted the buyout option. It was careful to hawk the company around in order to pre-empt any criticisms from the shareholders about the sale price. Although circumstances looked so adverse, Dennis's optimism and persistence proved a decisive factor for the success of the buyout.

Conclusion

'Managers are the power base, finance is only a commodity', declares the chairman of a highly successful bought out company. It is at this stage of the buyout that the leader of the buyout is assembling crucial managerial skills and abilities. The success of the buyout will ultimately rest on the vendor's and the financial institutions' faith that the business is being sold into capable hands. Unlike other typical post-buyout problems, such as squeezed cashflow, poor quality management is one of the few things that cannot be remedied. If the buyout is to succeed, the team leader has to select the right people first time round.

2

Preparing the Proposal

Having established with the help of its advisers that the business or division is a viable target for a buyout and that the vendor is willing to consider such an option, the management team must now begin working in earnest to prepare a feasibility study. The study, which can be used later as the basis for a financial proposal, must be a comprehensive and objective assessment of the management team's ability to run a new business.

Although the team's advisers will have endorsed the likelihood of a successful buyout, it may be wise at this stage to make an informal approach to a couple of financial institutions to test their initial reaction. If the team suspects that the vendor will doubt its ability to raise enough finance for the buyout, it would be wise to approach financiers before broaching the subject with the vendor. A simple telephone call, giving broad details of the division or business and the probable price, is often all that is required to find out about financing possibilities.

Who you should 'phone is a more difficult choice. Picking a financial institution at random from the telephone directory could be a serious mistake, as a large number are still inexperienced in this area. They may give the team an unfavourable reaction for reasons wholly unconnected with the viability of the buyout. Their reluctance to consider investing may be because of their (unconfessed) limited technical know-how about buyouts. They can also have an investment policy which is generally unfavourable to buyouts. On the other hand, even if the team does not get an initial brush-off, these organizations can be so excessively cautious that they dampen the team's enthusiasm and confidence and waste precious time.

Make sure that you talk either to someone knowledgeable about buyouts or to a professional adviser who can point you to two or three institutions with experience in buyouts. Most major firms of accountants have specialists who can make contacts for you (but be careful not to use the company's own auditors!). In an appendix at the back of this book there is a comprehensive list of advisers and investors.

The Feasibility Study

The feasibility study should be a useful internal tool for the management team and the professional advisers. It will help the management team to develop its strategic and operating plans so that it can bring a clear and unified sense of purpose and direction to negotiations with the vendor and financial institutions. There is nothing worse than team members presenting different views to investors. The feasibility study will also provide much of the information which will eventually be included in the detailed proposal. This means that critical information can be gathered and much important thinking done before the momentum of the buyout gathers pace as negotiations begin in earnest.

The discipline of preparing a feasibility study should force the buyout team to base its commitment to the buyout on hard financial analysis, instead of the excessive optimism and enthusiasm which dominates so many buyout teams. The team must make dispassionate estimates about the future performance of the new business and identify the areas where key changes have to be made. In essence, this stage will be a time of serious consideration and a careful weighing up of strengths and weaknesses of the business.

In most cases, it will not be necessary for the team to consider how the buyout should be structured as this will be negotiated at a later stage when investors have confirmed their commitment to the buyout. For the feasibility study, it needs merely to predict the percentage of equity funding that the management team and other investors can provide. The balance of funding normally comprises borrowing at around 3 per cent above clearing bank base rate.

The feasibility study looks at income projections, cashflow projections and business strategy. The first two areas will be the most important as far as potential investors are concerned. Cashflow is particularly crucial and will show whether the new business' profits will be sufficient to service the level of gearing or to finance capital expansion and working capital. It is these factors that initially determine whether the buyout is feasible and put a value on the company or division.

Both income and cashflow projections should extend to the first two to three years of the bought out business and should be prepared on a monthly basis during the first year. It is often wise to insist that all the members of the management team are involved in drawing up the projections so that it is a multi-disciplinary effort. Very few of the team will have had total responsibility for the cashflow of a business before, so it is advisable that team members familiarize themselves with the process and gain an early grasp of the mechanics of the new business.

(a) Income projections

The management team should base this on:

- Profit after interest, which is subject to tax. This amount will depend on several factors, such as capital allowances and non-allowable expenses.
- Turnover, based on expected sales over the next five years. The team should describe how its marketing strategy will affect turnover.
- Cost of sales. In many cases, the management team will develop a new manufacturing strategy for the bought out company. Unit costs are likely to change and, since past margins will no longer be relevant, detailed costings will be required. Other costs of sales which are likely to change involve the way the product is marketed. Increased sales usually require higher marketing expenditure and this is particularly true of service-based companies.
- Overheads. A detailed analysis of overheads should be included in the plan, with key operating assumptions, such as employee wage scales, being made explicit. In general, the overheads plan should be divided up by function and by type of cost.
- Interest which will be likely to be payable on the debt finance of the buyout, in addition to further funds to finance expansion or increased working capital.

(b) Cashflow projections

Almost without exception, it would be folly for these projections to be prepared by someone with no experience in this area. Even when using an experienced person, the team should consider employing an independent accountant to question the figures, challenge the team's notions and identify any 'blind spots', such as errors or inconsistencies. It is, after all, far less embarrassing and damaging if these are spotted by an external accountant rather than by potential investors.

Cashflow projections should be based partly on the figures for the past three to five years. The team should ensure that these figures are available, as banks and financial institutions are bound to scrutinize them very closely. Forecasts should be given in round figures of 100 to 1,000. A wise principle to remember is that projections should always overestimate rather than underestimate cashflow needs. Teams should take heed of the common problem of early cashflow crises in bought out businesses, which arise largely from high gearing and significant cash requirements for dividends.

According to accountants Spicer and Pegler, a number of important factors are often overlooked by buyout teams when drawing up cashflow forecasts. These include:

- accelerated cashflow because of creditor pressure immediately after the buyout
- debtor collection periods extended
- the cash consequences of a build-up of stock, or cyclical sales patterns
- set-up costs, including commitment fees from bankers and institutions. In the case of asset purchases, VAT will affect the purchase price on cashflow, although a VAT concession will be available in some situations
- capital expenditure requirements
- corporation tax liabilities.

It is all a bit like buying a new home. If you have to stretch yourself to the limit for the purchase price, you will find life very difficult as a host of unexpected smaller bills for such items as repairs or telephone connections come rolling in. It is easier all round for the team if it prepares cashflow projections via computer on a spread sheet programme such as Lotus or Supercalc. The greater detail that can be generated by the computer model may prove decisive during negotiations. As well as drawing up 'optimistic', 'realistic' and 'pessimistic' projections to cover all contingencies, the team has the ability to respond very quickly if any of the terms of the deal change at short notice. A computer model will also allow the team to test its assumptions by doing 'what if?' exercises, something the investors would require accountants to do.

A word of warning. Potential investors will make short work of projections which seem to be based on wishful thinking. Underpinning almost every projection will probably be a number of unstated assumptions and forecasts. It will strengthen the team's position considerably if it identifies these assumptions, substantiates them and improves their accuracy. The team could also build narratives on individual topics, such as administration and working capital, on to the projections. Marketing should be strongly emphasised as this has an important influence on almost every other function of the business.

Potential investors will also pay particular attention to more sensitive assumptions, such as the speed at which debtors pay, the time the company takes to pay its other debts, stock carrying levels, selling price and quantities and interest rates. It is important that the team estimates all of these as accurately as possible. A helpful exercise is to adjust cashflow forecasts to show the effect on cash requirements of different assumptions. Past history will normally present a good guide. Avoid the temptation to assume automatically that you can do better. Better be pessimistic rather than optimistic in your assumptions. For most businesses, payment within 45 days is optimistic, in 60 days realistic, in 90 days pessimistically realistic.

(c) Business strategy

Before formulating a strategy for the bought out company, the management team should make a commercial assessment of its prospects. This should include an appraisal of the likely demand for the business's product or service, sources and strength of competition and economic trends which may influence sales. The past performance of the business should be analysed to see if lessons can be learned and applied in the future.

The management team should ask itself a number of crucial questions about the strategic management of the new business. At this stage, the team will need to develop only broad strategies, but when it comes to present the final proposal to potential investors, it should have an extensive business plan. Some of the areas that investors will be concerned with are:

The marketplace:

- what is the company or division's present market position?
- can it realistically improve its market share through segmentation or innovation?
- what is the market size (is it growing or declining)?
- how is the market likely to evolve in the next five years?
- what stage has been reached in product life cycle (this applies to service industries too)?
- how strong are existing and potential competitors?
- what strategies are competitors using and how well do they react to any form of challenge?

The product/service:

- how is it used and how often is it purchased?
- how important is the brand name to customer loyalty?
- how highly does the customer value the product/service?
- how is product quality controlled?
- are unit costs sufficiently low?
- is there a dependable supply and is this flexible enough to cater for a changing market?

Corporate resources:

- what are the key labour/managerial and technical skills? How replaceable are they (supposing the technical director falls under a bus)?

- will the company need to buy in skill?
- what stage of the product/service's learning curve is the business at?
- what sort of profile and image has the company?
- what is the company's growth potential?
- what is the level of significant current assets, for example, plant, buildings, shares in other companies?

Initial Contact with Financial Institutions

Before the management team makes an offer and starts negotiations with the vendor, it should arrange a short meeting with two of three prospective financiers. It can use its viability plan as the basis for discussion about the likely success of a buyout and the level of funding required. As the financial institutions get a feel for the quality of the management team and examine cashflow predictions, income predictions, past performance and the background to the business, they will be able to indicate their interest in the deal.

Finding the right institutions to approach is an increasingly complex task. Managers are faced with a myriad of potential investors; according to the Peat Marwick database prepared for *The Financial Times*, there are no less than 137 providers of venture capital in the UK. Some 94 per cent of these have expressed their willingness to invest in buyouts. Added to these are the many financial institutions which have the ability to organize buyout syndications for virtually any sized deals. David Carter, partner of Peat Marwick, comments about managers' dilemma over which institutions to choose:

> In theory, they could send a worthwhile business plan to all institutions known to be interested; in practice their interest would be immediately dissipated. Yet the team which goes to only one institution will always suspect that it could have got a better deal elsewhere.

The compromise which Carter always recommends to managers is that, in the first instance, they select three institutions specializing in different aspects of buyouts, even though it may be necessary to replace one or more if they show no interest. 'This selectivity enables introductions to the institutions to be handled personally and allows the team to present themselves most effectively', he maintains. He does stipulate, however, that managers should seek objective advice, as financial advisers will be able to identify the key buyout players and may even have personal contacts with them.

The advice of David Shaw, director of 3i's management buyout division, is that, above all, managers look for institutions with proven expertise in buyouts. He also stresses the importance of compatibility with an institution and its whole investing philosophy. He comments:

> Financial institutions are very aware that they are no longer in a monopoly situation. They'll be selling to the management as much as the team will be selling to them. Managers should expect a 'beauty parade' of what services and facilities they can offer.
>
> The team should ask about the buyout deals the institution has been involved in and the sectors of business in which they are particularly experienced. The team should also ask about other deals, as some institutions may have backed a competitor. In this situation, managers should think carefully about working with the institution as it is necessary to develop very close working relationships during and after the buyout.

Ask yourself: 'Can we work well with these people? Will they give us the support we need? Would we want someone from this institution on our board?'

So who are the major investing institutions? Currently, the sector is dominated by a handful of institutions which have a considerable headstart in this field. Although each will say that it finances any type of deal, in practice each has a slightly different investment philosophy and preference for size and type of buyout.

Variables between institutions include the emphasis on the proportion of loan, preference shares and ordinary shares in the financing structure; who should have the majority shareholding, and the degree of involvement after the buyout. These differences depend partly on the likes and dislikes of the institutions, partly on the nature of the buyout. If the company acquires substantial assets, for example, and predicts a large profit early after the deal, the institution may put much of its money into redeemable loan stock.

Some of the other distinctions can be important ones. Take the use of ratchets, for example. A typical ratchet in a highly leveraged buyout might give the managers 15 per cent of the equity, rising to 25 per cent if they achieve operation profitability targets, or when the company goes to market. Ratchets normally require step by step improvements in performance to prevent a company from saving up all its best results for a particular critical year. If a company's performance is failing to reach its projected targets, ratchets can be used to reduce the management team's equity shares and increase the investor's. This way of using ratchets is strongly condemned by some financial advisers and institutions.

David Shaw, of 3i, shares this distaste. He explains: 'I personally don't like using ratchets because I feel their effect can be destructive and divisive. They can have a bad influence on the way managers run a business. They can, for instance, delay essential capital outlay in order to boost profits.' On the other hand, some institutions defend them strongly because they reduce the risk for the investor and act as a powerful incentive to the management team.

The major financial players

Currently, the buyout market is dominated by a small number of financial institutions. They are highly experienced in handling buyouts and have carved specific market niches.

Investors in smaller buyouts

The smaller end of the buyout market is occupied by a handful of institutions which until recently have enjoyed a monopoly in financing small deals. Although a number of institutions are now keenly competing for deals, the major players are still:

- Investors in Industry

3i was a pioneer of management buyouts in the middle 1970s when each buyout had to be approached, it says, 'as a journey with only the roughest of maps'. It has a formidable track record in this area. Peat Marwick estimates that the total value of 3i's investment in buyouts totals £140 million, making an average of around £700,000. It is probably the market leader for smaller sized buyouts and has a network of 23 regional offices.

In general, 3i prefers to take a minority equity stake in smaller buyouts. The organization is also taking an active role in larger buyouts. It increasingly leads and manages syndicates of investors, and tries to ensure that no single investor has a majority shareholding. It has recently been a co-investor with the Prudential Assurance Company and Murray Johnson, both major investors in this area.

In Carter's opinion, 3i 'places more emphasis on incentivizing managers than the miraculous financial effect of high gearing'. The organization itself describes its approach as 'taking as much account of human factors in sensitive negotiations as the money aspect'. 3i encourages management teams to approach it at an early stage in the buyout and is willing to discover on the team's behalf whether the company or division is for sale and whether the price is realistic. It will act as a go-between in initial approaches to the vendor and participate in negotiations.

- Moracrest

This is jointly owned by Midland Bank, British Gas Central Pension Schemes and the Prudential. Moracrest generally invests equity finance and has a policy of confining its investment to a minority stake.

Dedicated funds

The number of dedicated funds catering for large buyouts involving several millions has increased rapidly in the past three years. These include the Electra Candover fund (£260 million), Schroder Ventures (£72 million), Foreign and Colonial (£20 million), and Granville, which is aiming to raise between £10 million and £50 million. Granville's fund concentrates on the small to medium sized buyout. Charterhouse has also set aside around £100 million for buyout investments.

- Electra Candover Partners

Electra and Candover established this fund at the beginning of 1986 because they believed that a number of opportunities existed for buyouts costing over £50 million. Many such buyouts were being hindered, however, by the need to assemble substantial funds at short notice. The problem was compounded by the fact that these funds would in all likelihood have to be supplied by several institutions. Obtaining their firm commitment, as well as holding negotiations between so many organizations, made the deals almost impossibly complex.

Electra Candover aimed to circumvent these difficulties by establishing a sizable fund of around £260 million. It looks for large businesses with well established markets and products and experienced management. An additional criterion for the fund is that these types of businesses have the potential to be floated or sold in a relatively short period after the buyout. The fund charges the buyout team a transaction fee of 2.5 per cent of the total amount of the funds invested, including intermediate funding but excluding bank funding. At the time of writing, the fund has not yet invested in a buyout.

ECP's investment criteria include the provisos:

- that even in an economic downturn, the business should have stable and growing profits and positive cashflow to service loan and share capital
- key management positions should be held by experienced managers with operational, planning and financial skills
- the new business's existing borrowings should have been discharged or be capable of being assumed by the investee company
- the business should either have a significant competitive advantage in its market, or occupy a well established and preferably unique market position
- the business should not have any significant contingent liabilities, such as underfunded pension funds.

Investors in larger deals

The latest development in this area has been the arrival of a number of financial companies from the US leveraged buyout market. Already large players in the US, they have brought with them a wealth of experience and are offering a number of new lending techniques, which could lead to higher levels of gearing soon. These institutions include Citicorp, which has a fund of around £100 million for buyout deals, Bankers Trust, Security Pacific, First National Boston, Morgan Guaranty and the US Prudential Insurance.

- Citicorp Venture Capital

Citicorp venture capital, part of the US investment bank Citicorp, tends to concentrate on medium to large sized buyouts, especially those involving the buyout of a UK subsidiary of a US corporation. Its £100 million fund of equity finance is the first of its kind to be launched by an overseas bank in the UK.

Some of the buyouts led and syndicated by Citicorp include TIP Europe, bought for £60 million from Gelco Corporation; Cundell Industries, bought for £12 million from the Lawson Mardon Group; and Maccess, purchased from Burmah for £12 million.

Besides its emphasis on a quality management team and a secure market position, Citicorp's investment policy also includes:

- a low debt-to-equity ratio, allowing significant leverage in the new capital structure
- a proven earnings record
- strong prospects of stable and growing profits and positive cashflow to service debts, even during adverse economic conditions and inflationary cost increases
- an efficient cost structure and verifiable low production costs within the industry
- surplus or under-used assets
- proprietary products or services which are stable or predictable – this almost certainly excludes products exposed to rapid technological change.

- Electra Investment Trust

Electra concentrates almost exclusively on large buyouts which are likely to be brought to the market as soon as possible. Between 1980 and 1985, Electra has invested a total of £22 million in 23 buyouts, 10 of which were organized by Candover. During the five-year period, out of the 13 buyouts organized by Electra, three of these had achieved a listing, two had been sold off and the value of the remaining eight had increased by a total of £2 million. The trust has net assets of around £235 million and looks to invest only in sums of £75,000 upwards.

- Candover

This is partly owned by Electra and was established in 1980 with the principal aim of investing in large buyout deals. Between 1980 and

1985, the company has invested in 13 buyouts in the UK, including DPCE Holdings, Stone International, Vickers da Costa and Famous Names.

When making the initial approach to financiers, the management team should resist the temptation of playing off a number of institutions against each other. Such a practice is generally frowned upon and once word gets around (as it quickly will in such a small industry), the team may find its proposal dropped like a hot brick.

The banks' role

Although banks are generally intersted only in low risk ventures, one of the advantages of involving them in the buyout is that they are not looking primarily for high returns in income and capital terms but for interest on loans. This leaves the other investors and the management team to divide the equity stake between them.

Clearing banks interested in participation in buyouts include Barclays Development Capital, the Bank of Scotland, County Bank, Midland Equity Group, Lloyds Merchant Bank. Barclays Development Capital concentrates on deals of up to £5 million and has put some 80 per cent of its money into buyouts. It was the lead investor, for example, for the National Freight Company and the British Victualic buyouts. The Bank of Scotland has built a niche for itself as a secured lender to buyout companies. County Bank tends to prefer deals mainly involving debt capital.

The banks will require the same type of information as other kinds of investors and will be just as concerned with the viability of the buyout and the quality of the management as anyone else. Banks will, however, assess the risks of the venture more rigorously. This will involve an analysis of the commercial risks of the business, the quality of earnings and cashflow cover available and the spread and nature of assets and liabilities. Although security over assets is not essential, most banks will look for this as a guarantee that the high level of gearing can be supported. But what will be considered essential is the control procedures which are implemented after the buyout. Most banks will insist in addition that a regular reporting system is established, and that a rigorous and comprehensive set of covenants and ratios are set up.

Colin McGill, senior manager of the Royal Bank of Scotland, supplies the following profile of the ideal type of buyouts which many banks look for:

The company should:

- have a good track record
- have an established market share or niche
- be a net cash generator
- have a broad product or customer base
- have quality management
- have a developed operational infrastructure
- have established and efficient financial control and reporting systems.

The industry should:

- not have a substantial technological or research and development requirement
- be composed of stable markets
- include mainly UK-based operations
- be secure from the threat of competition from imports or alternative products
- be free of major disruptions caused by labour or supply problems.

The buyout deal should:

- give the management team a meaningful cash commitment and equity stake
- involve established, professional financial and advisory institutions
- build in comfortable initial liquidity levels and adequate financial resources after the buyout to ensure operational flexibility
- be based on a reasonable price/earnings ratio, and take into account goodwill

- contain comprehensive warranty and indemnity clauses in the sale and purchase agreement
- be subjected to a full accountant's investigation and independent consultant's report.

How are banks likely to react to the various different types of situations in which buyouts occur? Typical scenarios are:

(a) Buyouts with good asset bases but poor or suspect performance, and prospects of an improved performance after the buyout.

This type of buyout often includes companies about to go into receivership, or operations or subsidiaries divested from a parent company in financial trouble. Here, the banks will want to see good asset and security cover, combined with reliable control and monitoring systems, to compensate for the uncertain trading performance. Management teams must be prepared for banks to be concerned about over-gearing on the back of assets and the possibility of serious cashflow problems. Because the gearing may be high, the managers' equity share is likely to be low.

(b) Buyouts with reasonable asset bases and profit records.

These buyouts include strategic divestments of non-core operations or subsidiaries, and companies undergoing privatization. In these circumstances, banks would expect the sale price to be at or above net asset value to reflect the quality of earnings. Their lending assessment would involve a balance between cashflow and asset cover.

(c) Buyouts with strong cashflows and weak asset bases.

Most buyouts in the service sector would probably fit this description. Banks would most likely concentrate on the quality and predictability of cashflow and would expect the gearing to be modest with a fairly short loan repayment period.

Establishing a Broad Price Range

All too often, managers are unaware of the value of their business and end up paying far too much, especially if the vendor is a skilful negotiator. Ian MacPherson, of the British Linen Bank, has frequently seen management teams accept the asking price of the vendor without properly investigating the value of the business themselves. He comments:

> We might have a team approach us to provide finance for the vendor's asking price of £50 million. But you look at the thing and it's only making half a million a year. 'What are you paying so much for?' we ask and all they say is that it's the price the parents say it's worth.

As the management team talks informally with the vendor, professional advisers and potential investors, the likely price range on which negotiations will be based should begin to emerge. At this stage, all the various parties will be discreetly sounding each other out: the vendor will be trying to assess how serious the management team is in its intention and the extent of its financial backing; the management team will be trying to assess the vendor's reaction and its likely asking price.

In buyouts where the parent company or receiver is in a strong bargaining position, the management team may immediately be given a sale price and have little scope for negotiating. In cases where the vendor is more concerned with being assured that the management team will have the backing of financial institutions, a broad price range may be established at a later stage of the buyout. The final price of sale will be agreed only after a detailed proposal and analysis of the business have been presented to the financial institutions.

The terms of the sale will substantially depend on the circumstances of the buyout. When a buyout is the only possible option, or the value of the business is heavily dependent on the management team, a discount on book value should be obtainable. If the business is likely to be liquidated, or is in a declining market or industry, the price should be based on net realizable value. In increasing numbers of buyouts, however, the price of the business is based on the earnings potential of the assets. Buying at a discount on book value is becoming less common as buyouts involve fewer ailing or bankrupt businesses and more strategic divestments of profitable businesses. This trend makes it all the more difficult for management to scoop a bargain. Increasingly, they have to make sure they are on their toes and that they are prepared for a hard round of negotiations. This means they have to have a good sense of the value of the business before they agree a broad price range with the vendor.

The management team should avoid at all costs the temptation of acquiring the business at any price. It will have paid too high a price, for instance, if the net revenue generated by the business is not enough to cover interest and dividend payments. Net revenue should be assessed in terms of what is left over after working capital, funds for research and development and fixed asset replacements (which can be particularly heavy when the business has been starved of investment by its former parent company) have been deducted. One-off additions to the net revenue, such as grants, should not be included in the assessment, as these are only short-term boosts to the company's income.

Before determining a broad price range with the vendor, the management team should try to achieve a position of strength by looking at the buyout from every conceivable angle and by assessing its own bargaining power. The last thing it should do is to allow the vendor to believe that he holds all the trumps. Even if this is true, the vendor's complacency can be lessened by a management team which is plainly considering a wide range of options and which is quite ready to start its own business, should the buyout fail.

Establishing a price range is a psychological and tactical process. The buyout team should balance its own bargaining tools against the vendor's. Can any of the vendor's reasons for considering the sale be turned to the team's advantage, for instance? Who else could buy the business? Does a buyout offer any advantages over other types of sales? How valuable is the management's input into the business? The team should also consider how it could make the terms of the buyout more attractive to the vendor, by perhaps offering some equity or share options; or a guarantee of a continued purchasing relationship (Mecca, for example, agreed to continue to buy its beer from Grand Metropolitan as part of its buyout deal).

Valuing the business can be done using three main methods: earnings value, dividend share and asset value.

(a) Earnings value

Using this method, the value of the business is based on its predicted future earnings, after tax, depreciation, dividends on preference shares and interest have been deducted. The next figure to calculate is the price earnings ratio, which is the price of the shares divided by the earnings after tax. The assumed annual earnings after tax are then multiplied by the price earnings ratio. In some situations, the purchaser will use the P/E ratios of other companies in the same sector of business for comparison.

Using comparative ratios in this way can lead to serious inaccuracies, however, as P/E ratios can be calculated differently. For quoted companies, most P/E ratios are calculated on the basis of the actual level of tax which the company pays. For unquoted companies, P/E ratios are calculated on a notional (or fully taxed) basis, a method which is used by most venture capitalists. On this basis, the taxation rate assumed to be deducted from the pre-tax profits is the Corporation Tax rate.

The arguments against using this form of evaluation in a buyout are particularly strong. A valuation based on future earnings will be skewed if high gearing results in heavy interest payments. Another objection is that P/E valuations are virtually meaningless for companies which are trading badly. If these businesses have no publicly quoted companies to compare their P/E ratio against, this form of evaluation becomes even more difficult. Potential investors may also be reluctant to depend on earnings evaluation because of the possibility of declining profits after the buyout.

(b) Dividend share

Like earnings value, this form of evaluation is based on the company's future earnings. If a dividend is a fixed amount, the value of a share should be calculated on a dividend yield basis.

(c) Asset value

This is when the value of the business is based on the market value of its assets. With the exception of companies going into liquidation, goodwill is also included in the asset value calculation.

In most situations, but particularly when the vendor's asking price is very high, managers should remember that the terms of payment can often be negotiated to their advantage. Depending on the pressures on the vendor for payment, the team may be able to agree that a proportion of the price be paid over an extended period, say in five to seven years time. Such an arrangement would allow the team to raise its bid if a rival bidder enters the scene.

To ensure that an advantageously priced deal emerges, it is essential that the team makes good use of its financial advisers. Valuing the business and identifying the best price offer will often involve complex legal and tax calculations, especially if the company or division is heading for liquidation or receivership. The team's adviser can calculate the net returns to the vendor from these types of sales, compared to a buyout.

In the case of liquidation, the costs incurred make it likely that this form of sale yields far less than book value. Costs, tangible or otherwise, include:

- redundancy costs
- losses on plant and machinery which are probably sold well below their book value
- if a subsidiary is liquidated, loss of goodwill and damaged morale in the rest of the group
- damaged credibility to the parent company
- substantial stock losses when production or sales cease
- bad debts
- contingent liabilities, such as penalties on uncompleted contracts
- continuing overheads as liquidation is in progress
- continuing management costs as assets are sold off and the business is wound down
- deferred taxation costs.

3

Obtaining the Finance

Steven Bruck, of Pannell Kerr Forster, warns: 'Managers should expect a rigorous scrutiny from potential financial advisers and investors. Before they commit themselves to the team, they will want to form a total view and get a sense of the team's motives and track record. If an operation has performed badly, they will want an explanation and a demonstration of the team's achievements during that period of trading.'

Approaching financiers with a detailed proposal

Financial institutions receive hundreds of proposals a year, with fewer than 5 per cent being accepted. Whether the management team truly has the ability to buy a company or division successfully will become clear during its discussions with potential financiers. It must convince institutions of its professional ability to run a business and put together a comprehensive, persuasive and well presented business plan. Much time and care will be needed, but by this stage the team should have already developed a feasibility plan on which it can base the detailed proposal.

Even before it presents a detailed proposal to financial institutions, however, the management team has a substantial advantage over other prospective propositions, particularly start-up projects. On the whole, management buyouts have been traditionally much safer forms of investment. Compared to a one in three chance of failure for a start-up venture, approximately one in ten of large buyout deals (for companies costing over £1 million) fail, while for smaller buyout deals the failure rate is one in eight. Statistically, buyouts show a much better rate of return. On the whole, investors prefer backing a venture where the management is already in place, the product or service is already tried and tested, and where less 'hands-on' attention is needed.

The buyout proposal has a critical influence on the success of the venture. Managers should remember that once a financial institution agrees to supply finance, it is just as committed to the business as they are. Like the management team, an institution will become a shareholder and will have a vested interest in ensuring the business is healthy and profitable. If the two groups are to form a strong partnership, the management team should not use the proposal as a tool to whitewash or dress up the company's performance. The proposal should be an open and frank description of the business which allows an institution to assess exactly what are the risks involved and to grant its commitment unreservedly to the venture. Any skeletons in the cupboard should be admitted and strengths and weaknesses discussed honestly.

The function of the proposal is to:

- establish the credibility of the buyout team
- outline the future management and direction of the company
- be a major tool for assessing the strengths and weaknesses of the management team.

The financing proposal

Broadly speaking, the proposal should include a description of the background to the buyout; look at manpower and financial resources; include key marketing information; analyse past and future performance; describe and evaluate what is being purchased; examine the past and future organization of the company. It should be concise, attractively bound and be around 15–20 pages long. Any additional financial information and detailed calculations (if the proposal is to be convincing there should be plenty of supporting documentation) can appear in appendices to ensure that the main document does not become a heavy and unreadable financial treatise.

(a) *A brief introduction and list of contents and appendices.* The introduction should explain the reason why the buyout proposal has arisen and its main characteristics. Does the buyout concern an independent company still trading, for example, or a company going into receivership? Is it a subsidiary? Is it the purchase of assets from the vendor, or the purchase of a company where the management team already owns some shares? It should describe the strengths of the business and say why it will be a successful venture.

The introduction should indicate briefly the amount of funding which will be required and sum up concisely why the business is worth investing in from the investor's point of view. The whole section should be only between one and two pages and should allow the financier to get a 'feel' for the buyout. It should be brief, easy to read and contain just enough information to interest but not to swamp the reader. The management team should remember that this is the section where potential financiers will make the choice of either dismissing the proposal or reading on.

(b) *The background to the buyout.* This should look briefly at the history of both the buyout unit and the vendor company, its origins, owners and directors, products and services. The proposal should outline the nature of the target business' relationship with the vendor, its degree of autonomy and dependence on the vendor for services and functions. The background to the target business should outline its origin, date of incorporation and trading, details of inventions and provisional or final patents.

With the help of a financial adviser, the team should outline the amount, type and combination of finance needed, such as secured or unsecured loans or equity shares, and the length of time of repayment. These requirements should be neither over-generous nor underestimated. The latter is more common and arises from the risky assumption that the financing can be supplemented at a later stage. Deliberately underestimating requirements can also make the team appear financially naive.

Any reports from independent advisers about the feasibility of the buyout should be included, although these can appear in the appendices. The proposal should also describe the risks of the buyout and the possible actions the team can take to minimize these.

(c) *Manpower resources.* For many of the potential investors, the quality of the management team will be the target business' most important and valuable asset. This section, one of the most crucial in the entire proposal, should give a thorough description of the track record of each manager in the buyout team and his or her knowledge of the industry and market. Past successes, relevant experiences, examples of effective strategic planning, the ability to cope with stress and respond positively to change, should all be heavily emphasized. Whenever possible, managerial strengths should be expressed in such a way as to emphasize the strength of the team as a whole, rather than to suggest a reliance on an individual.

A general description of the whole workforce should follow, including a brief career description of key employees who are not part of the buyout team and the level of trade union activity. The team should describe the current number of employees and state whether and how it plans to expand or decrease the number. If any sites are to be closed, the proposal should estimate closure costs including redundancy payments, holiday pay and pension rights.

(d) *Financial resources of the target business.* This should describe long-term capital structure and shareholders; taxation aspects and working capital, including the detailed debtor and creditor position. Other relevant information includes the size and terms of any loans from both external sources and from the parent company; details of the target business' bank, financial security arrangements and borrowing limits.

(e) *Key marketing information.* This should analyse the state of the market in which the target business is trading, the market's size, growth potential, stage of maturity, and the key competitors and their market share. If the target company is operating in a declining market, the management team should seriously reconsider the feasibility of the buyout. It may be useless to try and convince potential investors that dynamic and entrepreneurial management will compensate for this weakness. A financial adviser asserts: 'If the target business is trading in a steadily declining market with a mature product, financiers will not believe that the company will be able to show good or even outstanding results, no matter how good its management.'

The product or service should be described, with particular attention to any special or unique features. Product or sales brochures with illustrations could be included in the proposal, and a description of any past or future research and development. The team should outline its marketing strategy and how it will implement it, including pricing strategy, export opportunities, orders in hand, sales contracts and seasonal trading characteristics. It should describe the business' suppliers and state the customer base.

If the latter is too narrow, it should indicate whether it is possible to broaden it, or whether it can receive an assurance from a major customer of continued business after the buyout.

Overall, the team should demonstrate its knowledge of the market, its awareness of opportunities and its strategic ability to exploit these.

(f) *Trading performance*. This section should provide a summary of the past five years' audited accounts; production and sales records for the past five years; a break-even analysis; gearing and sensitivity analysis and a profit forecast for the first three years of the buyout. Cashflow forecasts for the next two years and a statement of assumptions on which the forecasts are based should also be given. This statement should be very thorough as banks will rigorously examine the accuracy and reliability of the assumptions. Areas of doubt and margins of error should always be stated. Details about financial security can also be supplied, but the team should not be over-concerned with this as profits and cashflow projections are far more important. Wherever possible, the team should emphasize its financial know-how and careful financial planning.

(g) *What is being purchased*. This should include details of fixed assets, stocks and work in progress. The proposal should describe existing premises and plants and the size and condition of office, production and storage areas, including rates and rents. If the premises are leased, information should be given about whether this is a full repairing lease and if it can be assigned. Maximum production levels, the amount of staffing required and the life expectancy of all the various assets should be estimated. Details of patents, copyrights and trademarks should be included in this section.

(h) *Past and future organization*. A clearly understandable organization chart should be provided, plus an assessment of the effectiveness of the current managers and their ability to control the target business. The team should state how it will manage the new business, including its plans for accounting controls, speed of reports and variance controls.

Motivation

Not everything that potential investors are looking for will be reducible to a set of figures in the proposal. Potential investors will also be concerned with the team's motivation and reasons for a buyout. According to Stephen Bruck, of Pannell Kerr Forster, four basic motives often underlie buyouts, all with varying degrees of acceptability to investors and advisers. These are desperation, ambition, frustration and opportunism.

(a) *Desperation* – often felt by managers about to lose their jobs because the operation is about to go bankrupt or be sold off.

'Managers feel forced into doing something that doesn't come naturally', says Bruck, 'essentially, you are dealing with a negative situation, where problems can arise during negotiations'. Managers may be blinded by desperation, for example; they may be incapable of managing a bought-out company, or they may take irrational decisions about how to structure the new business. Says Bruck: 'Desperation is not a firm foundation for a buyout. Potential investors would probably react negatively if they knew the members of the management team were desperate to save their jobs.'

(b) *Ambition* – 'one of the best driving forces', which meets the full approval of financial advisers. 'There's nothing wrong with ambition – that exactly describes the attitudes of the investing institutions and their expectation of a 35–40 per cent compound return', points out Bruck.

Almost every financier and adviser knows of a similar situation to the one experienced by a leading financier. He found in his office one day a middle manager who was determined to fulfil his youthful ambitions of becoming a millionaire. 'Like thousands of other ambitious MBAs, he became a line manager. As time passed, he almost came to the point of abandoning his ambition, but as he approached middle age, he suddenly asked himself "why the hell aren't I working for myself?". That's when he came to me to negotiate a buyout.'

(c) *Frustration* – often felt by managers in a business that is being held back by its staid or inefficient owners, or which is part of a conglomerate and which does not fit into its mainstream activities. The ownership may be unsupportive, repressive, inward-looking or inflexible. Says Bruck: 'Frustration is a fair motive, but it should contain some seeds of ambition too'.

(d) *Opportunism* – arising in managers who recognize an opportunity for success, or who have been asked by the owners to buy the unit or company. Although opportunism is a positive motive for a buyout, financiers will want to be sure that the management team has a vision for the future of the business.

Obtaining an agreement, in principle, to provide finance

After presenting institutions with a detailed proposal, the management team should not expect anything more than a verbal confirmation of interest. The current law of enticement which applies to UK divestments restricts the type of investment which the financial sector can make. Institutions can be accused of enticement if they offer finance freely and with initiative. Until there is a clear indication of a willing vendor, these organizations will be reluctant to offer anything more than verbal assurances.

Conclusion

This stage of the buyout is the most exhausting and time-consuming for the management team. As well as assembling a plethora of financial and management information, the team must make an imaginative leap and put itself into the vendor's shoes. Managers should be clear about why they want to do the buyout and be prepared for both potential backers and the vendor to grill them about their motives. They should also be prepared to be asked whether they have got their family's support; many managers of successful buyouts stress the importance of an understanding and supportive family. Lastly, the management team should not underestimate the buyout's disruptive impact on the business. Someone on the team should be given special responsibility to act as watchdog over the company and to allay the uncertainties of anyone connected with the business. This precaution ensures that the team returns to a business with customers, suppliers, employees and, most importantly of all, a future.

4

Negotiating the Deal

The buyout now enters its most crucial stage, with all the main players poised for action. The vendor has agreed to the possibility of a buyout and has endorsed the price range on which negotiations will be based. The full management team is in place, with a backup of professional advisers who will examine minutely the legal and tax details of the deal. The initial commitment of potential backers has been gained and a lead investor has probably been identified. Failure at this stage will exact a heavy penalty on the team, both financially and personally.

Negotiations can take anything from three weeks to two years, depending on the complexity of the deal and time pressures. In all likelihood, they will be tough, intensive and very exhausting. A manager comments:

> The buyout is a lengthy process; ours took around six months, with the later stages being especially time-consuming. We went through hard, but always fair, negotiations with the vendor and were pressurized by the threat of other bidders. You must remember all through the buyout not to neglect running the business. You must also reassure the work-force and key customers of the buyout's progress.

One of the contributory factors to the slowness of many buyout negotiations is that the investors are simply not used to moving rapidly. Of those managers identified by our survey as dissatisfied with their advisers, 25 per cent complained about the slowness of their decision-making (see appendix 3).

The various concerned parties will be determined to get the best deal possible, but in many cases the management team is in the weakest bargaining position. The experiences of the chairman of one bought out company will be familiar to many managers. He comments:

> We were faced with a stark choice: an 'out of the blue' order to close down or to organize rapidly a buyout to protect 50 jobs. The reason for the closure was that our parent group was being sold to an American company which did not want our subsidiary. Because negotiations for the group sale were well advanced, our chairman set a price for the subsidiary and gave us a 30 day timescale to complete the buyout.
>
> We had little time to consider. The existing three-man buyout team met to consider, made a few phone calls and then embarked on a 30 day race. Our chairman was not worried about closure costs and would not negotiate the price or the timescale. It was take it or leave it – so we took it.
>
> Many people think that buyouts consist of ordered negotiations with logical conclusions, but I am afraid this assumption is not very relevant to the real world.

Even when the team is negotiating to buy a business going into liquidation, the bid's success is by no means guaranteed. Receivers or liquidators tend to drive a hard bargain and are highly capable, experienced negotiators. Their overriding consideration is to get the best price for the business, and they are rarely swayed in their approach to the negotiations by the fact that the bidders are managers of the business. The team will find the terms of the deal will probably be quite severe, with most receivers insisting on a cash up front payment and the purchase of all the assets of the business.

As far as the financial institutions are concerned, there are plenty of other promising deals to back, especially in the present booming buyout market. They will often strike a hard bargain with the team by attempting to gain as much equity as possible and by looking for handsome returns. The managing director of a bought out company whose owners were retiring is sharply critical of his backers. 'Our main problem was the attitude of the institutional investors', he says. 'We found they rarely understood how the market operated and often had too high expectations of return on investment.' Another director of a bought out company dealing in magnetic components found that some investors expected his team to make crippling financial commitments. He recommends: 'If the banks or investors want personal guarantees in addition to a second mortgage on your house, don't hesitate to find some other investors'.

In many cases, the careers of the team will hinge on the success or failure of the buyout. If the vendor is hostile to the buyout, its failure may endanger the team's continued employment.

Even when the buyout has been initiated by the vendor, the stakes can be total. 'It was a take it or leave it situation', recalls the manager of a successfully bought out company. 'We were told to either lead a buyout or have the entire business closed down'. Another manager comments: 'We always knew that if our parent company rejected our buyout offer and accepted a bid by a major US competitor, it would be only a matter of time before all of us in the management team were replaced by US executives.'

Even when they know their positions will still be there should the buyout collapse, these managers run the risk of being unable to adjust back into the old groove. After experiencing the excitement of coming so close to being independent, returning to the restraints and controls of the normal managerial role may be intolerable. Another danger is that they may feel their professional reputation has been damaged by the failure of the buyout, making it impossible for them to stay in the company.

For some managers, the consequences of failure may even mean financial ruin. A manager in a medium-sized company had seen the profitability of the company that he had founded plummet after its sale in 1979 to a major client. 'The client had wrecked my company. Some 18 months after the initial sale, I decided the only way to save the business was by repurchasing it. I risked personal bankruptcy to mount a management buyout.' In the event, his gamble paid off and the company is now showing healthy profits.

Unfortunately for the management team, negotiations for the buyout are made considerably more risky by the absence of any binding agreements from financiers to provide backing and from the vendor to sell. Often, the team is in a 'Catch 22' situation of being unable to receive a firm financial commitment from potential investors until they have a clear indication of the terms of the sale. The vendor, however, will often refuse to give these terms, or even to draw up a price range until it is confident that the management team has adequate financial resources. As it wants to get the best price for the business, the vendor may also delay declaring its terms until it has some idea of the extent of the capital that the team has access to. If both vendor and backers are wholly inflexible in this area, the buyout can sometimes come to a crashing halt, which can prove expensive in terms of paying professional fees, many of which are calculated on a time basis.

This impasse can sometimes be resolved by obtaining broadly written agreements. The management team should ask its solicitor to investigate the possibility of drawing up a conditional agreement with the vendor, which will be the basis of negotiations. The team then has something definite to show to backers. Any problems about the price of the deal or the terms of the sale can be identified at this stage, allowing the team to return to the vendor and change the contract. A letter of intent may be an even better option for the team. Using legal help, the team can draw up a concise and non-legally binding letter of intent which it can exchange with a similar document from the vendor.

Another option is for potential investors to supply the conditional contract, but a major drawback of this is that one of their conditions will be inevitably that backers must agree to the purchase price. This means that at any stage of the negotiations, the backers can withdraw from the deal. It will only be when the entire deal is signed and sealed that the team can be confident that the buyout has succeeded.

Bargaining with the Vendor

Who should negotiate?

Are managers the most obvious and suitable candidates for conducting negotiations? Not necessarily. In the majority of cases, the decision to acquire a business is based on objective corporate or financial strategy. While these factors figure in buyouts, many complex pyschological factors also come into play. A problem is that the management team can feel at a psychological disadvantage negotiating with its bosses. The team may also be propelled by personal motives. For example, ambition, idealism, greed or desperation may be the driving forces behind managers' commitment to a buyout.

The vendor can also be prey to similar forces. It may support a buyout because it is the quietest and least embarrassing way of selling the business, for example; or it may be hostile to the buyout but be forced to acquiesce by the threat of a management walkout. Inviting a third party to participate in negotiations can sometimes be a valuable way of diffusing many potentially explosive situations between the team and the vendor.

Steven Bruck, of Pannell Kerr Forster, maintains that it is often better to prevent the management team leading negotiations with the vendor. He comments:

> When the vendor turns round and asks for an unreasonably high price, it can be emotionally very difficult for the management team to turn its back on the deal. Often, the vendor is very aggressive to the team and takes the attitude that if the team is going to walk away from the deal after all that time and preparation, it needn't bother to work for the company any more. The emotional blackmail which the vendor can exert over the management team can be terrific.
>
> Once they have made the necessary mental switch and started down the buyout road, managers can become desperate if they think the buyout will fail. They become willing to pay any price.

A buyout financier maintains that the management team should be kept away from the negotiations at all costs. He comments:

> Although the team can be tough as they need to be in business, they can become as pliable as babies during negotiations with vendors. One reason is that sometimes they're scared off by the scale of finance in a buyout. I always recommend that the management team allow either the lead investor or a financial adviser to conduct the bargaining. Their personal money isn't at stake; they can be tough during negotiations and walk out if the vendor becomes unreasonable.

Typically, negotiations are shared among backers, advisers and the management team. Of those financial institutions which feel strongly that the team should negotiate, the typical reason is that 'if it's not capable of heading negotiations, it's not capable of running a business'.

How to negotiate

The Economist's *Guide to Management Buy-outs* provides a checklist of dos and don'ts for the management team. These include:

- Formulate negotiating tactics

Before any meeting takes place, the team should select a leader and prepare for the meeting. It should have a clear idea of the vendor's weaknesses and strengths and the considerations influencing its decisions. The team should try to prepare some answers to the vendor's likely questions and use role-playing exercises. It should also consider any objections or counter-proposals and decide which managers will tackle specific areas. How, for example, would the team react if it was told at that stage that negotiations were going on with another bidder, or even another buyout team? To what extent could the team afford to improve its terms if a competitor had just tendered a better price for the business? This leads to the next point – that the team should:

- Review major negotiating points

The team should clarify the salient issues of the deal and identify areas where compromise is possible, areas which are non-negotiable, and areas which are less clear-cut and which the team may need time to consider. This prevents the team from making any rash decisions, or becoming too inflexible. It also lessens the likelihood of negotiations reaching an unnecessary deadlock; the team can allow the other side room for manoeuvre in less important areas of the deal.

In the buyout of Aerosols International from Cadbury-Schweppes, the management team was adamant that it would not pay much over £3 million. Cadbury was pushing hard for a price that was six or seven times earnings, but the team resolutely stuck to its limit. 'By this time, County Bank were doing the talking for me and they were very good', Tony Wardell, the head of Aerosols International, told *Business World*.

- Match the buyout team with the vendor's team

It is important that the two negotiating sides are psychologically balanced and that neither feels bullied. The buyout team should try to discover who and how many people will represent the vendor. It should tally the number of its members with the vendor's, and try to match technical and managerial skills. It should also consider whether any personalities will clash.

- Prepare for meetings

Build in enough preparation time before each meeting and find a meeting place which allows discussions to go on as long as necessary. The team should be prepared for meetings sometimes to be very protracted, but it should also take steps to draw meetings to a close when views are being repeated and no useful progress is being made.

- Conduct positive negotiations

Throughout the negotiations, the team should emphasize areas of agreement, rather than continually drawing attention to points of disagreement. Often, it can be useful to identify these areas of disagreement and, assuming that they are not fundamental, agree with the vendor to put them aside and get on with more central issues. These items can be returned to, once the main terms have been agreed. After meetings it is useful to circulate minutes to all the parties concerned, which clarify outstanding issues and which help to show how compromises may be reached. Minutes of this kind are also a way of avoiding misunderstandings.

- Take a break

If discussions become heated, or if a difficult decision needs to be taken, the team should not hesitate to call for a short break of 15–30 minutes to allow each side to discuss the contentious issue. The buyout team should never openly disagree with each other, but can use these short recesses to iron out difficulties and work towards restoring a united front during negotiations.

Agreeing Terms

Sale of assets or shares?

There are broadly two choices for transferring the ownership of the business. The most common arrangement is to buy the assets of the operation, which include plant, premises, stock and goodwill. The advantage of this is that the buyout team can select specific assets, leaving the vendor with the problem of disposing of worthless or superfluous assets.

Buying the assets allows greater scope to the team for claiming capital allowances against future tax liabilities, which lessens the risk of hidden liabilities. Potential liabilities from such things as old contracts and taxation can also be left with the vendor. Most importantly, the team is free to employ key personnel only, as this form of acquisition does not require employment contracts to be automatically passed on to the new owners. This means that the vendor is forced to give a redundancy payment to every employee. The team, on the other hand, is free to issue new employment contracts to whomever it pleases.

Another increasingly popular practice is to buy the shares in a company which owns the assets. In almost all cases, the vendor will prefer to sell the company as this is a simpler sale method which minimizes his tax liabilities, such as capital gains tax. This form of purchase entails the transfer of all employees, trade agreements, patents, contracts with suppliers and customers, licences and trademarks. One disadvantage is that, unlike a single sale of assets, assets which are transferred with a company in this manner do not qualify the team for capital allowances. Another disadvantage is that the liabilities of the acquired company also become the responsibility of the new owners.

Negotiations will be heavily influenced by tax considerations for both parties and the management team should make sure that it has evaluated their significance before negotiations are fully under way. Some key tax differences between buying assets and shares include the following:

- Tax losses – these cannot be passed on if the management team buys the assets of the business. If it buys the shares, however, it acquires tax losses which can be set against future profits if the business continues to trade in the same area for three years after the change of ownership.

- Capital gains – when assets are sold, the vendor must pay corporation tax on chargeable gains on goodwill and premises. When the business' shares are sold, the vendor must pay corporation tax on chargeable gains arising from the disposing of shares.

- VAT – when assets are sold, VAT is charged on taxable assets.

The sale of shares is, however, exempt from VAT, although the new owners may be liable for the former owner's VAT debts.

Hive downs

If the vendor favours selling shares, it may be necessary to hive down selected assets to a wholly owned subsidiary. This enables capital allowances and losses to be passed on to the new subsidiary without any immediate tax liability.

Whatever options are considered, it is crucially important that the management team has some idea of how the vendor is likely to react to its offer and the conditions of the purchase. The hazards of misunderstanding the vendor were seen all too clearly in the collapse of the £49.8 million buyout of Molins, the maker of cigarette manufacturing machinery, in September 1985. Apart from the Haden Group, the Molins deal was the first attempted buyout of a publicly quoted company. Molins' profits had been declining in the last few years; its profits of £12 million in 1978 had shrunk to £6 million in 1984, with the next year seeing only a small upturn to around £8 million. Towards the end of 1985, the company had warned that trading conditions were not expected to show any real improvement and that long-term survival depended on the success of its new products under development.

In the light of this performance, the buyout team's offer of 170p a share, which was 18p above the price of the company's shares just before the buyout was announced, might have seemed reasonable. But what most of the City and Molins' institutional shareholders realized was that the company had substantial future potential, given the chance to rationalize and to dispose of assets. The quality of its existing management, especially under the leadership of Christopher Ross, Molins' widely respected managing director, was another major bonus. Undoubtedly, the share price at the time of the buyout offer was in no way a true reflection of the company's value.

Molins' institutional shareholders were also aware that, should the buyout go ahead, the new company would probably seek a flotation on the stock market in the future at a much higher share price. 'The venture capital funds are not in this deal for charitable reasons', was the hostile comment of one of the company's fund managers.

Unfortunately for Molins' management, the example of the buyout of Stone-Platt, the engineering company, was pointed to as an example of how a buyout can profit venture capital organizations at the expense of virtually everyone else. Amidst great opposition from the management, the buyout of Stone-Platt ended with the company going into receivership in 1982. Many of its businesses were successfully broken up, while the core of the company, Stone International, was profitably refloated in 1984.

In the event, Molins' institutional shareholders, which included M & G unit trust group and the Prudential Assurance, rejected the buyout offer. Not only were they dissatisfied with the share offer, but they also gave short shrift to the team's justifications for a buyout. The argument that becoming a private company would give Molins the same degree of confidentiality enjoyed by its major competitors, who were already private companies, was sharply dismissed. One major institutional shareholder claimed the team's argument was 'nonsense. In such a restricted market, it is inconceivable that your rivals do not know about your activities'.

The collapse of the Molins' buyout is a warning against alienating institutional shareholders and causing them to question the underlying motives of the buyout. It is also an illustration of how a management buyout often precipitates the team and the existing shareholders into an immediate and obvious conflict of interests. Perhaps if the low bid offer for Molins had not aroused such a heated response from the shareholders, the buyout team and its backers might have been able to negotiate more acceptable terms. As it was, the buyout offer was sharply and irrevocably rejected.

As one leading fund manager commented to *The Financial Times* at the time: 'The bottom line is that if there are going to be Plc buyouts, the management must make damned sure the shareholders are being given maximum value for their interests.'

Additional sources of funding

- The vendor

Although a rare event, the vendor will sometimes help finance the deal, either through retaining a long-term minority stake in the business, or through deferred payment over a number of years. It may also help in the short-term financing of the business through an overdraft arrangement, leasing of equipment or a sale and lease-back agreement. Whatever the arrangement, maintaining a relationship with the vendor can be very beneficial. For example, in the early stage of the buyout short-term parental support, both in terms of financial and functional resources, may be crucially important.

In its first flush of independence, the management team should not throw out the baby with the bath water by automatically severing all links with the vendor. But if it does decide to maintain a relationship, it should be aware of the danger of the vendor interfering with the team's corporate and marketing strategy. If the vendor still has a trading link with the business, interference becomes even more likely. For instance, the team can encounter opposition if it attempts to lessen its dependence by broadening or changing its customer and supplier base.

- The employee

Inviting employees to participate is another option which can sometimes have spectacular success, as the buyout of National Freight illustrates. Either staff have a small equity stake through an employee share scheme, or the buyout is totally employee-led. Considerable sums can be generated through either arrangement; in the case of National Freight, for instance, the workforce of 26,000 raised £6.5 million to fund the deal, with the banks putting up the balance to reach the sale price of around £53 million. Around 30 per cent of employees each subscribed £700, by no means a huge sum of money.

Employee participation has been hindered in some degree by the need for secrecy during negotiations. If the vendor wants to dispose of a business quickly and with the minimum publicity, it will oppose any involvement of the rest of the workforce. If there are several bidders for the business, the vendor might interpret the management team's overtures to the workforce as a way of blackmailing it to agree to the buyout. Although the practice is widely condemned, management teams have been known to deliberately flout the vendor's wishes for secret negotiations by canvassing for the workforce's support, and then using this as a bargaining tool with the vendor. But if redundancies are an inevitable outcome of the buyout, employees will be hardly likely to give their financial support.

Other hindrances to employee buyouts are the legal restraints which affect companies undergoing a change of ownership. One way for employees to buy a stake in the new business is to use the redundancy payments paid to them by the vendor. This arrangement is not always possible, however, as some companies will fall foul of Transfer of Undertakings regulations, which contain a number of clauses to protect people working in a company which is being sold off. If the operating unit or company qualifies for these regulations, the team may find that it has to guarantee continued employment to all employees. This means the vendor escapes paying redundancy fees.

If this is the case, the management team may be able to persuade the vendor to lower the sale price. Another way of aiding employee participation is to make use of the 1981 Companies Act which allows companies to give loans to employees to enable them to purchase shares. Tax relief is also now available on these types of loans, although qualifying companies must be at least 75 per cent employee-controlled.

Mike Rogers, the head of the British Nursing Association, maintains that 'far too many buyouts involve only half a dozen top people'. He comments:

> This is not a real buyout to me. All middle management should be involved and share options issued for every employee with at least a couple of years experience should be put in place within a reasonable period. This is harder work, of course, and limits the equity slice of the top people, but I could not have been happy if our buyout had involved any other type of arrangement.

The management team which expects trade unions to welcome an employee buyout may be in for a rude awakening. Although this situation may be changing, trade unions have traditionally resented employee buyouts. Their objections are frequently that:

- Buyouts, whether initiated by management or the workforce, almost inevitably mean that redundancies will occur.
- Employee buyouts mean that workers are putting both their savings and their jobs in the same risk basket and stand to suffer heavy losses if the business fails.
- Trade union membership tends to fall as traditional wage bargaining functions are less relevant.

- Employee ownership in a buyout is short-lived, as the ultimate aim of the buyout is some form of exit, be it through a sale or listing. This means that ownership will once again return into the hands of external shareholders.

International research by Keith Bradley, of the London School of Economics, and Alan Gelb, of Harvard Business School, has found that employee buyouts are by no means trouble-free. Although some buyouts show instant improvements in productivity and performance, many go through a troubled period, once the initial euphoria is over. Bradley and Gelb comment: 'The main challenge to management in employee-owned business is how to prevent the deterioration of labour relations once the honeymoon is over.'

A major problem is that management fails to adapt to the new pattern of shareholding and, in the eyes of employees, does not allow them enough say in decision-making. In a medium-sized company in the United States, employees became so frustrated at their lack of influence over policy and management's refusal to concede wage increases that they made corporate history by becoming the first employees in the USA to strike against themselves.

Bradley and Gelb point out that worker-owners are not so concerned with routine high-level management decisions, or with day-to-day dealings with suppliers and distributors and are, in that sense, 'reluctant managers'. Of much greater concern to employees are managerial decisions which are task-orientated. Employees often wish to introduce practices which improve productivity and product quality. Another key area where employees demand to be consulted is corporate strategy, which particularly includes acquisitions, divestments, substantial investment, changes in product lines and the impact of new technology.

If they are thinking of an employee buyout, managers should carefully consider the impact on industrial relations and their own management style.

Potential problems

Negotiations are often complicated by the many difficult and emotional decisions which have to be made. Some redundancies will have to take place, as will negotiations with trade unions about employees' rights, obligations and working conditions. For its own sake, the management team should not depend on the good will of the workforce, but ensure that every agreement is discussed and put in writing. Nothing should be left to chance, as one buyout team discovered to its cost. The managers' belief that employees were content with the buyout arrangement was shattered when the entire workforce called a strike only 24 hours after the sale was agreed. The managing director of a printing company recalls:

> The first two years of our buyout were very difficult financially. We needed to reduce staff levels to survive, which involved protracted and difficult negotiations with the printing unions. In hindsight, the redundancies were inevitable and should have been an integral part of the original buyout conditions.

Transferring pension rights can be a potential minefield, and the team should make sure it seeks professional advice. Pension rights are not legally transferred, so managers will have to do some hard negotiations with employees or trade unions. Whatever happens, employees must not feel that they are losing out from the buyout.

One manager has bitter memories of negotiations. He declares:

> My message to anyone contemplating a buyout is this: it must be thought of as a total war. No concessions can be made and it must have priority over everything else in your life.
>
> Our buyout was unusual in that the team consisted of several middle managers from the unit involved. We stipulated to the vendor as a condition of sale that the two top layers of management would not be acquired by us. The managers in these levels who were not in the team were subsequently removed by the vendor well before the completion of the buyout.
>
> This factor created a need for extreme secrecy in the early stages until the announcement by the vendor that the sale was under negotiation. In fact, the top man learned of our approach and made an unsuccessful competitive bid. The second senior manager of the unit knew nothing of the buyout until the announcement.

Seeking new premises is often another major problem. In the case of a company dealing in rubber products, the time and expense spent in finding a suitable site seriously jeopardized the success of the buyout. The management team was under heavy time pressures to complete the deal before the closure of its loss-making parent company. The subsidiary's factory site was not owned by the vendor, however. Says the chairman of the bought out subsidiary:

> The cost of relocation and refurbishment of equipment represented a substantial part of the financial package, and was the aspect that our financial investors were least happy with. To make matters worse, our new landlord delayed in making the premises available, which affected our performance in the first couple of years after the buyout. Negotiations were further hampered by the strong possibility that the vendor would cease production and withdraw finance, causing us to lose our market.

The buyout eventually succeeded, although the terms which were set by the institutions were not ideal and caused some early problems after the buyout. Despite its reservations about the financial structure, the management team accepted the terms, as it felt that it would be unlikely to find alternative funding at such a late stage.

Walter Gibbon's buyout of a BL-owned subsidiary was also dogged by the same problem. Gibbon had been brought in to wind up one of BL's manufacturing plants. A section of the plant, which had a small contract to supply London Transport with couplings for underground trains, could not be transferred elsewhere in the group. Despite an initially hostile reaction from BL, Gibbon was able to go ahead with the buyout of this section. But, by then, the operation only had four months before it had to start work on the London Transport contract, which contained heavy penalty clauses if production fell behind schedule. Gibbon and another colleague immediately ran into the problem of finding premises. Their first attempt to gain backing failed because of this; it was only when they went to 3i that they managed to convince the owners of a small industrial estate that they were credit worthy.

Even then, their problems were not at an end. The factory premises were still being built and would plainly not be completed in time to start production. 'We moved into the site while the buildings were still incomplete', Gibbon told *International Management*. 'For two weeks, we worked 19 hours a day, seven days a week to install the equipment.' Production started only a few days late, with the new company escaping London Transport's penalty clauses. 'If possible, consider as many options as available before you conclude the initial package', warns the company's chairman. Another manager of a buyout suggests that 'if you are looking for new premises, find at least three suitable sites as it is possible that your initial choice may not be available when the buyout is completed'.

Structuring the Deal

Capital structure

Structuring a buyout often involves stepping outside of conventional financing guidelines and employing a number of different methods. The combinations are innumerable, so the capital structure of each buyout tends to be tailor-made.

In most deals, the financial package will consist of a mixture of equity and debt. Financial institutions and the management team will share out between them an assortment of equity shares, while the loans will be in the form of long- and/or short-term debt, with either a floating or fixed interest rate.

The ratio between debt and equity will largely depend on the strength of the balance sheet. A structure which mainly consists of loan funding means regular fixed payments, while a bias towards equity funding means that dividends must be paid when the business is producing a profit. The buyout team should not instantly jump to the conclusion that equity funding is automatically the better option. Although the problem of repayment is delayed until a time when the business' profits have increased, the conditions attached to equity funding can be alarmingly severe.

John Coyne and Mike Wright, lecturers in industrial economics at the University of Nottingham, supply an example of how 'these types of shares can carry quite a sting in the tail'. They refer to one such arrangement, where preferred ordinary shares are entitled to a fixed cumulative cash dividend each year of 10 per cent of the total subscription price. After one year's grace, the management team must pay this dividend every six months. In the agreement, these shares are also entitled to a yearly cumulative cash dividend 'of such sum as when added to the fixed cash dividend shall equal 6 per cent of the net pre-tax profit of the company'.

It is crucial for managers to investigate the terms of investment fully, otherwise they may find the profits of the company severely drained.

Voting control for the management team

A fundamental principle for many investing institutions is that the buyout team's motivation and commitment to the business will be strengthened substantially if it has voting control of the business. But often the team's financial resources are limited in comparison to the scale of the bid, making it difficult for it to acquire voting control.

One solution is for the institutions to reduce their own equity share and increase unsecured debt funding, a method known as mezzanine funding, a mixture of equity and debt. The mezzanine investor is exposed to greater risk than usual as the ordinary debt provider takes security over the assets of the company ahead of the mezzanine provider. To compensate for the higher risk on debt, investors will look for a higher rate of return. Mezzanine funding is provided only if a business has a committed high-quality management team, good cashflow, or proceeds from asset sales.

Mezzanine finance, which originated from the United States, can be arranged in a variety of ways. One of its forms is as an unsecured debt with a much higher yield, supplemented with separate equity. This equity often consists of fixed participation rights, which entitle the investor to additional dividends in certain circumstances. The only drawback of this form of mezzanine is that servicing such a debt arrangement from gross profits can actually decrease the value of the business when it comes to be floated. Fixed participation rights also mean that the equity of the business is eventually diluted.

Another form of mezzanine capital is convertible, redeemable preference shares. This form of equity yields several benefits to the business and the investor. Redeemable preference shares are serviced out of net profits, giving the investor the benefit of taxed income. If the business performs well, these shares are redeemed, improving the market value of the business. If the business performs badly and the preference dividend is too great a drag on cashflow, it can be converted to ordinary shares. Using this type of mezzanine means the management team's equity share will be diluted only as a last resort.

Conclusion

Negotiations over the structure of the deal are likely to be complex and difficult. Even if the vendor and management team agree on broad terms, legal and taxation problems can act as a spanner in the works to bring the whole transaction to a halt. Discussions often seem to progress smoothly one moment and then seem on the brink of collapse the next. There will also be times when relations between the vendor and the management team become very strained. Through all this period, the only recourse for the management team is to have unflagging patience and persistence, and to take every step to ensure that the momentum is maintained.

5

The Buyin

Hard on the tail of the buyout is the concept of the management buyin – a mechanism which allows a team of outside managers, backed by a financial institution, to acquire control of a company. The buyin tends to be billed as a means of removing managerial deadwood, weighing down a business.

In an unfriendly buyin to a quoted company, it is up to the buyin team to convince shareholders that it could run the company more efficiently and that the shareholders would be better off. In the more usual case, top management of a group recognizes that it can get a better deal for an unwanted subsidiary through a buyin than an ordinary sell-off. The whole process is a form of revitalizing an ailing or under-performing business by grafting or transplanting a new team of owner-managers.

The buyin largely owes its birth to the increasing popularity of the management buyout and the recognition of the rich pickings that can be gained from successful deals. Managers and financiers have become less cautious and more willing to experiment with imaginative and unconventional methods of acquiring a business. When this new zeal is coupled with the development of sophisticated financing techniques, it is inevitable that businesses will begin to be bought and sold in more flexible and inventive ways. Considering the youthfulness of the acquisition 'industry', it may well be that management buyouts and buyins are only the start of a wide range of new weapons for takeover armouries in Britain.

There is no shortage of funds available for management buyins. One reason for this is that the recent boom in management buyouts has led institutions to put aside sizeable funds for such deals. But competition to fund good buyouts is now so severe that it is becoming harder for these institutions to find worthwhile buyouts to invest in. As a result, the institutions are considering the buyin option with increasing interest.

Dr Hugh de Quervain, managing director of Midland Montagu Ventures and a leading expert in buyins, expects the method quickly to become an established acquisition technique. He comments: 'The development of the buyin is almost a market reaction to a situation where the market is crowded. There is now too much money chasing too few worthwhile buyout opportunities.' In March 1987 de Quervain's company, which is the venture capital arm of Midland Bank, organized a conference on buyins which was claimed to be the first of its kind in Britain, if not in the world.

The gathering pace of acquisitions of all kinds is also indirectly fuelling buyins. Companies that want to divest some subsidiaries may prefer selling to an external team of managers, perhaps because it feels the existing management is not capable of a buyout, or because the technical and managerial skills of the team are too valuable to lose and need to be better utilized within the group.

Anthony Lunch, director of BASE International, a consultancy specializing in corporate development funding has found that 'large company frustration' often provokes managers into seriously planning a buyin. He comments:

> They may feel this way because their desire to buy out a division has been prevented by corporate policy. Sometimes it's because they have been unable to get their corporate bosses to accept an expansion policy, or it may be simply a desire to get together with a group of colleagues who have worked well as a team and 'do it again', this time 'for ourselves'.

Owen Williams threw up a 25-year career with IBM United Kingdom and a position on its main board when he was invited to head a buyin into MBS, a computer distribution company. 'My wife thought I was going through a mid-life crisis', Williams told *The Director*. 'We had enjoyed a very good lifestyle and now I was challenging all that. There was a look in the corner of her eye of "what's he up to?".' Williams has never regretted his decision, although he does not recommend the same course to everyone. 'I wouldn't give it as general advice to move from big companies, and the statistics are against it'. Running his own company has supplied a challenge which was lacking in the corporate board room. 'I wanted to do my own thing. I had to get it out of my system. I couldn't have spent my retirement saying "what if. . .?". Now I'm more interested and alive than I ever was before.'

A surprising number of successful buyins have already taken place, one of the earliest being the buyin of Cambridge Instruments in 1979. Other notable deals include the £310 million buyin for Woolworth Holdings, Meggit Holdings, Melville Technology, Cullen's and Barker and Dobson. Midland Montagu alone has backed 16 buyins since 1979.

The Target

Although possible, there is very little sense in buying into a company that is performing well. The target company's shareholders or owners will want to be convinced that the buyin team can make a substantial impact on the business' performance and will be unlikely to support a buyin that seems to do little else than disrupt operations. For this reason, a buyin makes most sense when it involves a business which is under-performing because of poor or unimaginative management. It need not be losing money, just not making the return on the investment required by the group.

For a buyin to succeed, the target company's vendor or shareholders must be convinced that the growth potential of the business has not been exploited. Ideal targets for a buyin will, therefore, involve companies where the management is entrenched in the routine day-to-day tasks of running the business. Typically, these management teams are concerned with survival instead of expansion and are following horizons that are frequently too short and too narrow. They may have a poor awareness of the market, be largely ignorant of the threats and opportunities of new technology, or lack the ability to open up new business opportunities, particularly on an international scale.

Specific targets for buyins include:

(i) Family businesses

Arranging a succession in family-run businesses is often a serious problem, which at the worst can lead to the company being broken up, sold or even liquidated. France's small business sector has been crippled in the last few years by owners retiring with no identifiable successors. A government study at the beginning of 1985 revealed that 65 per cent of France's small enterprises had no family successor. A tenth of all liquidations occurred because of a failure to secure a smooth transfer of ownership.

Often, a buyout is impossible because the existing management of the business, which may include some members of the family, does not have the ability to take over the reins, especially in a time of rapidly changing markets and technology. 'Many family businesses suffer from marketing and technology myopia', maintains Lunch. 'Having worked all their lives in one sector it is difficult for them to put their heads above the parapet to see wider opportunities. The company therefore tends to stagnate and decline'.

Selling out totally can be a hard choice to make for a family-run business. The family may have strong ties with the local community and developed a sense of responsibility which prevents it from selling the company, especially if there is a strong likelihood that the new owner will make redundancies or that the business will be removed from the locality. For many family-run businesses, a buyin will be the only acceptable option. A new management team can have a dynamic impact on the business and will be concerned about its long-term growth. The owners can gain some benefit from the increasing value of the business by relinquishing control only gradually. But if this is the arrangement, there should be some sort of agreement about the amount of freedom that the management team will have to implement changes.

Once the buyin is in place, the team will probably focus its attention on regaining the confidence and commitment of suppliers and customers and convincing everyone, including employees, of the healthy continuation of the business.

Risks

- If the basis of the relationship between the owner and the new buyin team is left ambiguous, tensions will probably exist while the former owner still has a significant stake in the business. The owner may find it difficult not to interfere with the team's decisions, while the loyalties of employees can be split between the old and new management. 'Much depends on personal chemistry and trust', says Lunch. 'In a case we are familiar with, the incoming team has established the level of confidence necessary to achieve control of board policy without having a majority of the shares, or indeed investing any cash initially.'

- A family which has run a business for several generations may advertise for a buyin but can, at the eleventh hour, be unwilling to relinquish its power and back out of the deal, at great inconvenience and expense to the buyin team.

(ii) Expanding entrepreneurial ventures

A buyin can be an excellent solution for an entrepreneurial business going through problems because the founder lacks management and financial skills to control its growth. Many promising new ventures are begun by an entrepreneur strong in technical expertise but weak in management. As the job of managing the business becomes more complex, the founder finds it difficult to accept that new skills are needed and that a management team should be formed. In some cases he or she may not necessarily be the most appropriate person to run the company. The entrepreneur may try to retain control at all costs and may even deliberately strangle the growth of the company.

Rather than relinquishing control completely, the founder/entrepreneur can invite a small number of carefully selected managers to buy into the business. If the entrepreneur ultimately prefers to be a 'big fish in a small pool' and is only truly happy working in a small venture, he or she can be freed to establish another start-up by handing over to the buyin team completely. The founder's exit route can be structured and timed in such a way as to benefit from any improvement in the company's value. If he decides to stay, the buyin should bring into the company managers with the skills and experience he lacks. A typical route might be for the technically orientated founder to bring in a marketing orientated chief executive.

Once the buyin has been completed, the team will probably concentrate on creating an efficient management infrastructure and monitoring and control systems.

Risks

There can be a serious cultural clash between the new management when it comes from large companies, and the existing managers and employees of a smaller entrepreneurial company. The buyin team may try to implement managerial controls too swiftly, and underestimate the strength of cultural differences. It may be necessary for the incoming team to be willing to adjust its management style for a while in order to ensure the smooth transference of ownership.

(iii) Ailing start-ups

BASE's Lunch describes these as the 'walking wounded'. He explains:

> Every venture capitalist has one or more: the start-up company that didn't quite make it; the exciting team with a novel idea that took longer to develop and was inadequately marketed; the company where the product was perfectly valid but where the management was just not as good as it appeared to be when it sold the investment to the fund.

Although a buyin is not the only option, it is often the one which costs the investor the least amount of trouble, time and money. Although selling the company would be a speedy solution, the full market value of the business would probably not be realized. Further money could be injected into the company, but would not be a guarantee that any problems would be solved. The investor could implement managerial changes by bringing in one or two additional people as employees, but a more effective way of doing this would be to invite in an entire management team. Giving them an equity stake in the business would dilute the previous management's share and leave the buyin team with a free hand to expand the business. In some cases, the original management team might lose their equity – and jobs – entirely.

After the buyin, the team will typically place a much heavier emphasis on marketing than on product development.

Risks

If the reason the company is not making enough of a return is because the market is not ready for the product, or is much smaller than predicted, the buyin team must be sure it really *can* do a better job than the previous management team.

(iv) Failed buyouts

The first couple of years of the bought out company's life are crucial, as the new management team juggles between expanding the business and servicing the funding debt. Inevitably there will be casualties as some management teams fail to get to grips with their changed responsibilities and tasks. Some buyouts will fail because the management team has overstretched itself and been unable to cope with freedom and independence. Others will flounder because the level of gearing has proved too severe and is crippling cashflow, inhibiting innovation and internal investment, and ultimately strangling the business. In other cases, it will be sheer bad luck – an unpredictable change in the market, the loss of a key team member, or the collapse of an important customer. Whatever the cause, a drastic deviation from promised performance will most likely damage investor confidence. Exchanging the management team and injecting new capital into the business may be the most obvious and sensible solution.

Melville Technology, a Letchworth-based maker of switches and electronic measuring instruments, was bought out from the machine tools group Alfred Albert in 1980. Two years later it started to struggle under the weight of its gearing. The company was the target of a £3.4 million buyin in the spring of 1985 by three former directors of Mowlem Technology (now Buehler International). These directors, led by John Poole, former head of Mowlem Technology and now Melville's chairman, had considered staging a buyout inside Mowlem, but had chosen the buyin as an easier and less time-consuming option.

Ironically, although Melville was performing well below its backers' expectations, it was nonetheless showing small but respectable growth, with profits increasing from £270,000 to £452,000 and sales rising from £6 million to £7 million between 1983 and 1985. Most attractively for the buyin team, Melville had just scooped a $9 million contract from Hauni-Blohm to manufacture metrology equipment.

'On its own admission, the buyin team bought a business which was in good shape, despite the long recession of the early 80s, and with a strong order book', one of Melville's former directors told *The Financial Times*, when he and the rest of the buyout team resigned after the buyin. At the time of the buyin, the business was enjoying lower interest rates and a better competitive position in US and West German markets because of currency exchanges than when the buyout occurred.

On all counts, Melville's performance could hardly be described as poor, nor could the buyout be considered a failure. But this is exactly how Melville's backers considered it. 'There was a mismatch in expectations', admits Malcolm Gloak, a local director of 3i, one of the two investors in the Melville buyout. 'The return that institutional investors needed for the size of the investment they had put in was manifestly not being achieved. The management did not do too badly, even if the company did perform dully.'

Now a new round of venture capital has been injected into Melville in order for the company to be bought again, this time for £5.5 million. Around £1.5 million of this was earmarked to fund the product development for the West German contract. External directors with the managerial and commercial ability to run this and other similar projects had to be brought in, and in order to improve budget controls, four new profit centres were created. But even if the £1.5 million is left out of the calculations, the company is still weighed down by a £4 million debt burden, compared to shareholder's funds of £1 million. The present buyin team hope to clear Melville's balance sheet by floating it as soon as possible.

Risks

- Although the buyin is still in its infancy, some early experiences suggest that many problems arise because of a team's inability to establish good relationships with suppliers and customers. Many of these will be nervous about the change of ownership and the increased amount of debt which this suggests the company is carrying. The buyin team will have to prove that it is better qualified than the previous management team to run the business and will have to restore a sense of leadership and direction to the company rapidly.
- Financial backers, especially if they backed both the buyout and the buyin, are likely to want early evidence that their faith in the team is justified. If they committed capital to the original buyout, they could be nervous about making a second mistake. They may

adopt a more hands-on approach and demand a greater level of monitoring.

(v) Quoted companies

Initiating a buyin of a quoted company, particularly when the buyin team's approach has not been solicited, is a far more risky and difficult process as it often involves selling the concept to a large number of individual shareholders. If the buyin is contested, the deal can, at the extreme, whip up the same tensions, recriminations and accusations as a hostile takeover. Bidders must be people with 'an inbuilt resilience to character assassination', declares BASE's Lunch.

> When the buyin is contested, the defenders will seek not only to attack the terms of the offer, but also to demolish the reputation or ability of the buyin team. They can return with a better offer, but if they lose points on the personal front in the first foray, they are wasting their time seeking a return bout.

The failed £173.4 million buyin bid for Simon Engineering, a Stockport-based process plant contractor, during November 1986, typifies the risks of using this method to acquire quoted companies. The buyin team was headed by Philip Ling, the managing director of the bought out Haden Group, and included Sir David Nicolson, former chairman of BTR and two non-executives, Norman Ireland, finance director of BTR, and Jon Moulton, managing partner of Schroder Venture Advisers. If the buyin succeeded, Ling was to sever his links with Haden. The bid was made through Valuedale, a specially created company, which was to be renamed once the buyin was completed.

The board of Simon Engineering was swift to condemn the buyin and question the motives of the buyin team. In its view, the bid was 'unsolicited and unwelcome'. The board claimed that the buyin made no contribution to the interests of the shareholders or the employees and was an opportunistic attempt, devoid of any commercial rationale, to acquire the company at less than the current price.

The reaction of the City and the media to the buyin seemed a mixture of admiration of the inventiveness of the technique and caution about the wider implications for the future of public company acquisitions. An obvious benefit of the buyin as an alternative acquisition method was that it seemed a way of avoiding the huge expense and uncertainties of a takeover. Only four months earlier, during July 1986, Woolworth Holdings had spent almost £16 million chasing off Dixons, which ironically spent only £11.7 million on the attempted takeover. 'Unfortunately, takeovers often have such a traumatic effect on companies that they will pay any price to rid themselves of a predator', says a merchant banker.

Ling and his team were also quick to point out other advantages of the buyin option. At the time of the deal, they stated to *The Financial Times:*

> The City's normal remedy for a stagnant company is to arrange a takeover. Companies like Hanson Trust or BTR come in and buy the company. That has worked as a concept, but there should be a different formula to revitalise a company other than by burying it in a large conglomerate.

Sir David Nicolson added a further defence of the buyin method by maintaining that: 'there is a mass of middle-of-the-road engineering managers who only perform at 80 per cent of what they should be doing. The buyin would represent an injection of dynamism into the middle and top range of UK managers.'

Ling and his team heavily criticized Simon's financial performance. The company's earnings per share had risen by only 9 per cent over five years, while net extraordinary losses had totalled £19.7 million over the same period. Simon manufactures food-processing machinery and water treatment plant. It also provides process plant, mechanical, oil and electrical support services. Pre-tax profits showed steady but by no means exciting growth. They rose from £24 million on turnover of £503 million in 1984 to £26 million on sales of £539 during 1986.

Part of the reason for this lack-lustre performance in the view of the buyin team was the management's haphazard acquisition policy and failure to develop a coherent corporate strategy. 'Simon Engineering has the feel of a company full of people with ideas but with a log-jam of management and strategy at the top', Ling told *The Financial Times*. 'We can provide a new shot of adrenalin.' The team hinted, however, that it would probably consider inviting some of Simon's existing board members to stay.

The buyin team claimed that it could fundamentally improve the company's profitability by applying strong management and financial disciplines. 'It's what we did at Haden, all commonsense stuff,' said Ling, who had already carved himself an impressive track record throughout the 1970s and 1980s for revitalizing staid businesses. At the time of the buyin, the Haden Group's recovery was considered to be completed. Ling had successfully sold off the group's UK building services operations to BICC, leaving a profitable and self-sufficient US metal finishing division. It is fair to assume that the stimulation of managing Haden had lessened enough to cause him to look around for other challenges. He admitted his taste for shrewd financial deals when he initiated the buyin. 'I'm not wholly a wheeler dealer or a line manager in industry. I find the combination of the two intriguing', he commented.

Ling and his team attempted to woo Simon's shareholders by structuring as attractive a deal as possible. The team made corporate history by breaking away from the more conventional practice of giving shareholders the choice between selling out completely or staying with a new and untested management. It offered shareholders payment in cash yet continued control of the company until its performance improved. Simon's shareholders would receive 180p in cash and one new unlisted Valuedale share, which had been valued at 100p, for each Simon share. Simon shares were trading at 220p just before the buyin bid was made.

Only when the holding company's share price had risen by 60 per cent would the buyin team and the financial institutions be allowed to take a combined 37 per cent stake. Ling, Nicolson and Ireland would gain a stake of almost 7 per cent in the business, while the financial institutions would take around 30 per cent. Until the share price had risen, the team and institutions would subscribe £1.4 million for deferred shares only, which pay no dividends. The institutions would also subscribe £19 million for 10 per cent redeemable preference shares.

This innovative structure aimed to quieten shareholders' fears about risking everything on an unknown management team totally unfamiliar with the business. Deferred control meant that the newcomers would not be able to own a single Simon share until they had proved themselves. Shareholders would be able to benefit from future growth and profits, as they would retain a significant slice of equity. The structure of the deal also meant that the company could retain its stock market listing.

Schroders, the merchant bank advising Ling and his colleagues, was responsible for the idea of deferred control. Its venture capital arm, Schroder Ventures, led the investment syndication, which included Citicorp Venture Capital, Globe Investment Trust and Electra Investment Trust. Most of the finance was to come from Citicorp, as £100 million of loan capital and £6 million of equity.

In the event, Ling failed to persuade the City or Simon's shareholders that he was offering a good enough financial deal or stronger management. Simon's management strongly contested the bid and continued to claim that it would not tangibly benefit the company's shareholders and employees. Although the reasons for the failure of the buyin are not fully known, it is widely believed that shareholders felt the buyin team and its backers were taking too large an equity stake as their reward. Another contributory factor was probably the uncertainty about the value of Valuedale's shares. Although calculated by a major firm of stockbrokers, the evaluation would have to be ultimately based on the track record of the buyin team and its ability to fulfil its promise of improving Simon's performance. At the end of the day, the success of the buyin rested on a question of faith.

The timing of the offer did not help matters, either. With the City still reeling from the Guinness scandal, aggressive acquistion bids of any kind were unwelcome. Ling's attempts to play down the adversarial nature of the buyin were made fruitless by the unwavering hostility of the Simon board. Valuedale's case against the quality of Simon Engineering's management was also widely viewed as too weak, with the City favouring the verdict of innocent until proved guilty.

As the dust settles on Valuedale's failed buyin, it seems likely that during the current climate only agreed buyins into public companies will emerge. In many ways, the aborted venture was a test case for the acceptability of buyins into public companies. Its unsuccessful outcome is likely to deter similar deals for a while and encourage more deals supported or even orchestrated by institutional shareholders.

Richard Mead, the corporate finance partner at Arthur Young, recently commented to *The Times:* 'Hostile buyins are out of fashion. But I think there will be a number of put-ins, where we get smart management put in with institutional backing'.

Philip Ling is undeterred by his experience and convinced that, despite the unsuccessful example of Simon Engineering, buyins are now a permanent part of the acquisition scene in Britain. He comments: 'Leaving public companies aside, I'm sure there are going to be many more deals which bring together capital and new management to revitalize a company'.

Certainly not all buyins of public companies are doomed to failure. Ken Coates, formerly at Flight Refuelling and now chief executive of Meggitt Holdings, was more fortunate and initiated a trouble-free buyin of a public company as early as 1983. Coates and his colleague, Nigel McCorkell, were dissatisfied with their positions as directors of Flight Refuelling, a defence equipment company. Through a City contact, they came to hear that Meggitt Holdings, a machine tool distributor, was making a loss and might be a suitable target for a buyin.

Unusually for a public company, most of Meggitt Holdings' shareholding were owned by the management team, many of whom were approaching retirement. They willingly accepted the idea of a buyin because, as Coates explains, 'the company was in such poor shape that the managers were bound to welcome our arrival. There were no personality clashes. We did not see what we were doing as a new concept. It seemed the most obvious thing to do.' Since the buyin, which was backed by 3i, the company has returned to profit and has carried out a series of acquisitions itself.

Matching the Business with the Team

Already a number of merchant banks, accountants and venture capitalists are attempting to identify high-flying managers who would be suitable candidates for a buyin. In many ways, the potential buyin team has to pass a far more rigorous examination than its buyout counterparts. Because they will be strangers to the target company and possibly even to the industry, the team members' perceived managerial abilities will be crucial. 'A lot of money is going to ride on the ability of the management, new to a company and its business, to manage that company to great effect', asserts Midland Montagu's de Quervain.

Lunch believes that the qualifications a manager needs for a buyin are even more demanding than for a start-up. The buyin team has the difficult task of convincing financiers, the vendor and the shareholders that its abilities are valuable enough to saddle a business with a large amount of gearing. It must also be capable of rapidly increasing the profitability of a business as well as securing its long-term growth.

Lunch is regularly approached by 'consultants of the company doctoring kind', keen to invest time and possibly modest equity in a recovery situation. 'Although they may be useful in helping a company in solving specific problem areas, not many of them suit the criteria for long-term successful management', he comments. 'The same is often true for some middle management teams who have been persuaded by external forces, such as redundancy, that they are buyin material.'

In his view, the most essential trait is to have proven management skills. 'This is not the time to be claiming hidden or unfulfilled talents. You must have a clear winning track record in management and be able to project this and its significance to the development of the target company.' This requires someone adept at public relations who can also build a buyin team that has strengths so obviously lacking in the target business. 'The biggest single risk is that you, the buyin team, will fail to deliver', comments Lunch.

De Quervain identifies three essential traits of the buyin team:

- A proven track record of successfully managing companies, preferably, but not essentially, in the target company's industry. 'After all, a really effective general manager should be able to manage successfully just about any business', says de Quervain. Ideally, however, the managers should be familiar with the company's industry if they are to make as rapid an impact as possible on its performance.
- Experience of running an independent company. Running an independent business is often very different from running a subsidiary of a large group. Making that transition is difficult enough for many

buyout teams; it could become even more difficult for a team which has to adjust to working in a totally new situation. De Quervain comments: 'The ultimate ideal would be for the management to have successfully managed and sold out from a buyout situation in the same industry as the target company. An unlikely, but by no means impossible prospect.'

- A powerful will to succeed, both operationally and financially, 'MBIs, by their very nature, will make exceptional demands on the skills and determination of management'.

Once they have found a team, the managers and institutions work closely together to target a potential company. They do this in varying degrees of intensity. In some cases, the two parties pool their knowledge of the industry and use their informal contacts to identify suitable businesses. In other cases, they may use more formal methods. They may assemble available information from trade research analysis, the media and business and City analysts' reports, and form a database of businesses which are under-performing. These companies may be profitable, but be failing to fulfil their potential because of leadership problems, sleepy management, a defensive and reactive style of management, or because they are going through a period of strategic review.

Lunch's company works with managers in a variety of ways. One buyin candidate, for example, was a director in a large company in the metallurgy industry. He wanted to buy into a medium-sized engineering company in a sector with which he was familiar. Lunch's company helped to find a business which answered the director's specific requirements on location and the industrial sector. Another manager wanted to take on the challenge of running a medium-sized manufacturing company. He joined forces with BASE to find target businesses and to identify potential team members. A third buyin candidate had discovered three suitable businesses through his consultancy work. He planned to buy all three, but before he could make the offer, he needed help to develop a future acquisition strategy which would take into account technological developments. Lunch's company helped him to do this by carrying out market research.

If a financial institution is seeking to initiate a buyin, it will match its management team to a business using three sets of criteria. It will first look to see that the team has strong and complementary management skills. Next, it will consider whether the management team's abilities and experience precisely match the needs of the target company. Thirdly, it will look at whether the team is equipped with the right management skills to function in the target company's industry.

A large proportion of the managers identified by financial institutions as suitable candidates for a buyin are casualties of the recent spate of takeovers, and in the present climate, it seems likely that this easily tapped pool of managerial expertise will be the seed-ground for management buyins.

Philip Sturrock, former managing director of book publishers Routledge and Kegan Paul, is one such example. After his company was taken over in 1985, he became a consultant for a short time until he began discussing with the Prudential and Schroder Ventures the possibility of a buyin. Sturrock gained their agreement that if he could find a suitable company, they would provide the necessary funding.

After researching for six months, Sturrock and two other former directors of Routledge hit upon Cassell, a dictionary publisher and a subsidiary of Holt Saunders, the UK book publishing division of the US media group CBS. 'Cassell had a good name and a good backlist, but it hadn't realized its full potential', Sturrock commented to *The Times* recently. 'We moved in as a new top layer of management. We saw it as a business opportunity rather than a buyin.'

Negotiating the Deal

Management buyins are arranged using many of the same financing methods as for management buyouts. The buyin team will have to take similar decisions about whether to buy the shares or the assets of the target business. Minimizing the risk factor will be a more important aspect of the buyin than the buyout, however. The stakes are already high for the investor who decides to back a buyin team of people who may not have worked together and who are acquiring an unfamiliar business. A deal structure which minimizes risk will be a top priority, causing most backers to favour acquisition through assets rather than through shares. As with buyouts, buying the assets has the advantage that liabilities do not automatically pass to the purchaser, so that the risk of hidden liabilities is reduced.

For exactly that reason, the vendor may not be willing to sell the company through its assets, especially if the liabilities are open-ended and difficult to project on an accurate basis. There may also be difficulties in extracting the proceeds of the sale from intermediaries. Balancing sale charges and chargeable capital gains may also mean that the vendor is actually *unable* rather than unwilling to agree to a sale of assets.

Some fundamental differences exist in the structuring of a buyin and a buyout. These include the following:

(a) Venturing into the unknown

A key difference between the buyin and the buyout is that the buyin team has only limited access to information about the target company. The buyout team, especially if it is already running the business, has precise knowledge about the value of the company's assets, markets and manpower resources; the buyin team can only guess. This makes both the accountant's investigation and the legal details about material agreements all the more crucial in a buyin. On this count alone, buyins tend to be more risky than buyouts for the team and its backers.

Some of the risk can be reduced by asking the vendor for the usual extensive warranties and tax indemnities which are given in any type of acquisition of business and private companies. But not even this slight form of security can be obtained for the acquisition of a public company. The buyin team will have to base its negotiations on any available public information about the company. The only course for the team is to attach conditions to the offer, but these can only be on the terms that the sale will not proceed if the conditions are not satisfied.

When former IBM executive Owen Williams put his reputation on the line to lead a buyin in 1985 into MBS, at first sight the computer distribution company seemed an irresistible bargain. The buyin was at the instigation of MBS's chairman, Clive Richards, who offered Williams a sizeable equity slice as an inducement.

The only proviso was that Williams and his colleague, Stafford Taylor, another IBM manager, would not be allowed to look at the company's books until they had committed themselves to the buyin. The structure of the deal would be calculated on a profit forecast of £2–£3 million for 1985. It was only when everything was signed and sealed that the two men discovered that all was not as it appeared. MBS was almost bankrupt, despite a 100 per cent compound growth since its flotation in 1982, and a share price which had soared from 60p to 285p. 'The company had been run by seat of the pants management', comments Williams.

It took a substantial injection of capital and radical reorganization of property holdings and manpower resources to nurse the company back into good health. Williams set up IBM-style task forces which were assigned to tackle specific problems. Financial backers supported Williams' turnaround strategy by agreeing to a rights issue for £9 million. Then, just when the company seemed set for recovery, founder director Mike Brooke announced that he was selling his 5.5 million shares, an action which, after the rights issue, would swamp the market and almost certainly cause the share value to collapse.

A second, more conventional, buyin was the solution to this potential catastrophe. This would give Williams and Taylor the sizeable equity stake they wanted and prevent the shares from being diluted. Chase Investment Bank, which had originally floated MBS in 1982, bought the shares, keeping around two thirds for itself and giving the rest to the two directors. Chase agreed with Taylor and Williams that they would buy back blocks of shares at the end of 1987 and 1988 at cost plus interest. The bank's carrot was that if the share price improved, the two could make healthy profits by selling shares on the market before the first payment deadline. They would also have to relinquish less equity the higher the share price.

Because of their initial ignorance about MBS's performance and profitability, Williams and Taylor are caught in the usual high risk high reward buyin situation. 'It was a tough decision to go ahead with the buyin', admitted Williams to *The Director*. 'Most share schemes are options and have no downside. In this case, we couldn't avoid it. We've signed and we're held to it.'

(b) The risk factor

Acquisitions of any kind are a gamble, but the buyin is even more so for the management team. Managers will be expected to commit more personal finance in a buyin than in a buyout. Maggitt's Ken Coates, for instance, put £100,000 of his own money into the buyin in 1983. 'The buyin was a monumental risk', he admits, 'but it seemed just the right thing to do.' Because the buyin team does not have a proven track record with the company, investors and shareholders have to gamble on the personalities and abilities of the team. As one merchant banker points out:

> More than in any type of corporate deal, we are talking about investing in personalities. A hefty personal investment from the buyin team is very necessary to demonstrate its commitment to backers and the target company's shareholders.

The reputations of the managers are also at stake. Often occupying top management positions in major companies, the obvious question is why these managers are planning the buyin. Buyin teams cannot use the same justification as the buyout team that the bid is due to a strong loyalty and commitment to the well-being of the business. Greed is an accusation readily laid at the feet of the buyin team. A merchant banker warns:

> If you were thinking of such a course, your motives would have great bearing on your chances of success or failure. In the more public and contested cases, attempts may be made to demolish or vilify your reputation that could make the Greenwich by-election look like afternoon tea at the vicarage.

The existing directors of the target company may be even more anxious to scupper the buyin's plans. 'You have not only got to be determined, you have got to be tough enough to take and parry the fusillade from entrenched management positions', comments a manager. 'You may feel vulnerable, but don't forget the existing managers are being threatened with possible extinction.'

At the worst, the buyin team and the existing management can end up competing against each other. If an offer comes from an external team with no detailed knowledge of the business or even of the industry, it naturally occurs to the existing management team that it probably has just as good a case for acquiring the business. Contests between buyins and buyouts are likely to become a common phenomenon in the future.

The successful buyin of the dictionary publishers Cassell, for instance, came near to becoming an open fight between the buyin team and the existing management team. Sturrock and his two colleagues discovered only at a later stage that the management of Holt Saunders had considered an internal counter bid. If both CBS, the parent company, and Cassell itself had not backed the buyin, the outcome might have been very different.

(c) Voting control

Because the buyin is inherently more risky than the buyout, backers will often insist on voting control. When a publicly quoted company is involved, the team is even less likely to have control initially. This adds the further complication that the team may be prevented by other shareholders from generating cashflow through selling off assets, or by leasing back premises. This lack of control makes it crucial that the target business is not too highly geared.

Conclusion

The management buyin is an exciting variation to the buyout and an ideal method of acquiring businesses whose growth potential has been unexploited because of staid, lack-lustre management. In many ways, the buyin could give British management a welcome shake-up, and have the same long-term impact as that of the hostile take-over when it was first pioneered in the early 1950s. Whatever happens, the buyin is certain to be a permanent arm of corporate acquisition strategy.

6

On Your Own

A mixture of elation and exhaustion is often the first thing the buyout team feels after the deal is signed and sealed. After months of difficult negotiations and alternating waves of frustration and hope, the managers at last have ownership of the business. There will be little time for them to rest on their laurels or celebrate, however. In all likelihood, the business has been neglected for some months; employees will be uncertain about how the buyout will affect them; customers and suppliers will be looking for speedy reassurance that the business is in capable hands and will offer the same, if not better, quality of service as before. Before many hours have passed, the team must return to the nitty-gritty of running the business and start to make key organizational and managerial decisions.

What can the members of the buyout team expect to face during the first two crucial years after the buyout? Undoubtedly, their managerial abilities will be severely tested as they seek to justify the buyout through improving the business's performance and to service the new debt. The company's greater financial vulnerability means that the management team will be at the sharp end of business as never before. Every decision will count; the strategy it chooses, and the manner in which it is implemented, will quickly show whether the team has injected new energy and flair into the company.

Some buyouts, particularly if they are bought out subsidiaries, tend to show immediate and dramatic improvements. Being freed from the dead hand of corporate control often results in a surge of entrepreneurial energy and enthusiasm. Almost overnight, the external obstacles which prevent subsidiaries attaining their full potential disappear. Crucial decisions, on such matters as long-term investment or marketing strategy, which were constantly shelved by the parent company can now be taken by the team. The new company is suddenly free of group policies and overheads which either constrained it, or brought it few benefits. It can at last return to basics and concentrate on what it does best.

Paul Bion, majority shareholder of LogAbax in the UK, saw his company go from strength to strength in the first year after it was released from a major international company. He commented to *Management Today:*

> Subsidiaries get into trouble by following the directives of the parent, which are aimed at making the parent's accounts more attractive . . . In one year, we've more than doubled the turnover by concentrating on doing the things we're good at, not taking what the group said. We don't now have someone on the phone saying 'We've got 40 of these computers – you do want some, don't you?'

Another manager comments: 'Our overall business is better since it has been liberated from a parent company which was operating in a very different field. We are now able to take decisions as and when necessary'.

In the summer of 1982, Nicholas Mendes, a West Midlands public relations agency, commissioned a market research company to investigate how buyouts affect the performance of companies. It conducted personal interviews with 19 executives of bought out companies. According to the agency, all 19 of them believed their businesses had benefitted from being independent and claimed they were more successful, more effective and more competitive than they were as subsidiaries or divisions of larger companies.

The majority of executives said the buyout yielded the following benefits:

- improved loyalty and commitment from employees, resulting in greater efficiency
- increased flexibility, because of shorter chains of command
- improved performance, competence and motivation in the buyout team
- more rapid response to change in the business environment
- job preservation
- survival of the business.

One surprising discovery was that customers generally reacted very positively to the buyout. Far from creating uncertainty, the buyout seemed to generate much goodwill and sympathy among customers and few repercussions were felt in the market. Customers reacted favourably to the buyout because of their own increased expectations of the new business, particularly if it was a bought out subsidiary. They believed that trading with a smaller, independent business would result in greater flexibility, better service, faster deliveries and improved product range.

A small number of companies reported disadvantages from the buyout. One company, for instance, lost several customers because rumours of the buyout leaked out before transactions were completed. Fears about the buyout's viability led some customers to cancel orders. Pension arrangements were also a major cause of friction in companies, and many of the executives commented with hindsight that some of these difficulties could have been avoided if agreement about pension schemes had been reached with the vendor before contracts were signed.

One crucial problem area was the impact of the buyout on other managers in the business. Line managers were often given increased responsibilities, but sometimes they proved unable to cope. Poor decision-making at this managerial level was often a serious problem.

How Well Do Buyouts Perform?

Assessing the success of a buyout is a difficult task, as the definition of success clearly depends on the circumstances of the buyout. The managers of a company which has been bought out of receivership may consider the buyout an outstanding success if the company has managed to break even after a couple of years; similarly, the managers of a company, which showed great growth potential, may consider the buyout a failure if it does not match its original growth and profit targets.

Examples of failed buyouts are rare as investors and management teams naturally make every effort to dispose of the business discreetly, either by letting it go into receivership, or by selling off its assets piecemeal, as in the case of Stone Platt Industries, the failed textiles machinery company. Such clear examples of failure are rare, however, as most unsuccessful buyouts will be refinanced by renegotiating the long-term financial package, or sold off for the best price possible in the circumstances, or perhaps sold to a new management team.

Current research suggests that buyouts tend to perform well in the long term, although they almost all experience early teething problems. The buyout has a major impact on the performance of the company in terms of productivity, growth and profit. The performance of the buyout team is also affected, with both positive and negative results. Industrial relations also undergo some change, with some initial areas of strain surfacing during the early months of the buyout. Finally, the business's cashflow and financial resources will probably be severely squeezed under the new debt arrangements. Surviving these problems will be the first major challenge for the team.

(i) Performance

All the available evidence suggests that buyouts represent a lower than average risk for backers, and show better growth than generally expected. There is clear evidence that buyouts are less likely than start-ups to go bankrupt. Says a merchant banker: 'Management buyouts are much less likely to fail than other development capital situations, even though they are more highly geared. The better management performance after the buyout tends to balance out the risks.'

The survey of 111 bought out businesses by John Coyne and Mike Wright, lecturerr in industrial economics at the University of Nottingham, paints a positive picture about the performance of buyouts. Of buyouts which were older than two years, 38 per cent reported substantial stable profits growth, with the rest showing growth of some sort. Some 48 per cent of buyouts under two years old were reporting profits either slightly or substantially better than expected. Coyne told *Your Business:* 'Buyouts are performing well. They are doing better on average than similar companies during the same five-year period, and substantially better than any sample of start-ups.'

Some companies in the Nicholas Mendes survey reported greater productivity after the buyout. One respondent commented: 'Our productivity has risen by an average of 10 per cent, and 25–30 per cent in some sections of the company. We have cut down a tremendous amount of waste, including indiscriminate buying of consummables.'

(ii) The management team

The management team often undergoes a profound change of attitude after the buyout. A new sense of ownership is born among its members as they sample the fruits of independence and genuine control. Many teams become far stronger and more cohesive after the buyout. Individuals are welded into a team through the common bond of their commitment to the success of the business. If the team is headed by a forceful leader, the resulting strength and quality of management can be formidable.

For some teams, taking on new and wider responsibilities stretches individuals and brings out their full potential and abilities. An executive describes how the buyout has affected his team:

> The directors are now able to do things professionally with the business. We have improved the quality of manufacturing processes, built better relations with employees, got greater commitment from our managers, and have been able to make quicker decisions. We now have money available where necessary for making investment decisions.

Another manager describes the changes to his management team. 'The directors now have a sharper sense of perception. They are less compartmentalized and more aware of the overall aspects of the business.'

In Sebastian Green's report, *The Meaning of Ownership in Management Buy Outs*, one manager vividly described how the buyout changed his attitudes towards the business. He enthused:

> To actually take a £60 million company and implement all the ideas that you have for running that company, is an opportunity that comes once in a lifetime. The fact that you have had the dead hand removed creates a greater enthusiasm, a greater joy of actually doing the job . . . that in itself creates part of a sharper cutting edge.

Green's survey also found that management teams often have a greater sense of responsibility and accountability after the buyout. One participant commented: 'It is no longer possible to pass the buck upstairs. We are no longer corporate executives striving for recognition and promotion. Our achievements and failures are now self-evident.'

In some cases, however, some managers simply will not be able to cope with these new responsibilities and will find themselves out of their depth. In a number of cases there have been casualties during the early months after the buyout and the team will have the unenviable task of having to try to rid itself of unwanted managers. Buying out an owner-manager is a highly difficult and messy process.

The managers' sense of ownership and financial commitment to the business fundamentally affects its success. Coyne and Wright's buyout survey, for example, revealed that the managers' degree of ownership had a tangible effect on company performance. Among businesses where the buyout team had a majority stake, 44 per cent demonstrated a substantial increase in sales. Among those companies where the management had a minority stake, only 30 per cent reported similar sales increases. In this second group, there was a higher percentage reporting no change in sales.

But having a vested interest in the success of the company can sometimes inhibit team members and make them risk-adverse. It will be the task of the buyout leader to make sure that the team does not become over-cautious and too conscious of the high level of gearing. Finding a balance between being financially conservative but radical in approach to the market is one of the most difficult, but crucial, tasks facing the buyout team in the two years after the buyout.

Another major task will be to make sure that other managers do not feel alienated by being left out of the deal. Some degree of envy and resentment will be generated by the knowledge that the team will eventually reap handsome profits from the buyout. The team may find that all its efforts to generate new enthusiasm among managers are greeted with cynicism. It may well be wise for the team to provide some form of incentive for managers and other employees, which is directly tied to performance, such as profit-related pay, or a share option for when the company comes to market.

The management team must also make key decisions about how

the new company will be structured and how managerial responsibilities will alter. If the business is a bought out subsidiary, key functions must be replaced, either by buying in new skills or by using external support services.

After the buyout of Premier Brands, a former subsidiary of Cadbury-Schweppes, in 1986 the new management team made fundamental changes to the structure of the company and managerial functions. Paul Judge, the new head of Premier, split the organization into several clear divisions based on product lines, which included Kenco coffee, Typhoo tea, cocoa beverages and whiteners, and Chivers Hartley preserves. Each divisional director has largely been given his head to run his section as he chooses. Judge is introducing an aggressive marketing strategy and management style. He comments: 'We intend to set out clear corporate objectives, coupled with greater accountability. We want more "hands-on" management to cut out some layers of the corporate hierarchy. There has to be faster decision-making, with high achievers receiving recognition.'

Instilling effective management systems and controls will be a crucial task and a major factor in the long-term success of the buyout. Poor management systems were a major cause of the recent poor performance of Stone International, formerly part of Stone-Platt, a buyout which collapsed in 1982. Amid a blaze of publicity, Stone International was triumphantly floated on the Stock Exchange in 1984. Confidence in the management team ran so high that the company's shares were 18 times oversubscribed. Three years later, a series of disasters had caused profits to drop in one year from £6 million to around break-even. To prevent gearing from rising above 100 per cent, the management team was forced to sell off one of its most profitable subsidiaries.

What caused the company's performance to plummet so rapidly? Robin Tavener, Stone's hard-pressed chief executive, openly admitted that sloppy management controls were the major reason. 'We have been shooting ourselves in the foot', he explained to *The Financial Times*. The company's troubles started in 1985, when it won a major air-conditioning contract during a slack period of trading. The company accepted the contract, even though it meant a substantial cutting of margins. It went badly wrong, mainly due to the lack of a project manager. Large parts of the project had to be reworked twice. According to Tavener: 'We got the second design so badly wrong we couldn't believe it. The first four units of the project had to be scrapped altogether.' The division handling the contract was also hampered by managerial problems. 'We were not running it in a professional and systematic manner,' he commented.

Stone's US operations were affected by similar blights. Management problems in a normally profitable US subsidiary meant that essential equipment was missing. The completion of some major contracts was heavily delayed, causing Stone's yearly profits to receive yet another blow. Finally, another US subsidiary suffered a six week strike, resulting in 90 per cent of the workforce being replaced. Due to its inexperienced workforce and a depressed market, the subsidiary made losses of around £1 million.

All these disasters have severely dented Stone's credibility and thrown doubt on the present management's ability. The whole situation had led to an unwelcome resurrection of the memory of the collapse of Stone-Platt, which was mainly precipitated by the banks' refusal to extend the company's credit. Inevitably, questions are being asked about whether Stone International will follow the same route as its parent company.

The lesson to draw from Stone's misfortunes is that the buyout team cannot afford to rest on its laurels, no matter how positive the company's performance is during the initial post-buyout period. But how can the management team tell if its internal changes are working? After twelve months have passed, it can do some simple research and talk to people both inside and outside the company. It might ask some key questions, such as:

- what do customers, backers, employees and business observers see as the management team's strengths and weaknesses?
- how quickly are decisions made?
- does a consensus develop rapidly?
- how easily does information (particularly financial information) flow?
- are problems flagged up quickly or do most of the directors only find out about them at an advanced stage?

Although it is an area all too often ignored at the time of the buyout, the team should be alert to the eventual need to draw up succession plans. This is especially important if the team wants eventually to float the company, as any weakness in this area could damage its perceived value. One buyout backer points out: 'Buyout teams often range in age and motivation. What happens when the links between these people weaken? What happens when the driving force behind the buyout retires? Will there be succession problems?'

(iii) Motivation and industrial relations

'Without the buyout we would not have achieved what we did because the motivation would not have been the same', claimed Keith Meadows, head of computer maintenance company DPCE, to *Your Business*. 'After one year, we had many more customers than before the buyout. I had got in charge of the sales team and for the first time there was professional selling in the company. Before, we were a one customer company with a good, but diminishing, margin.' Two years after the buyout, the company was doing even better. It had been floated on the Stock Exchange and Meadows had become a millionaire. Profits were growing at an annual rate of 40 per cent and the company was about to expand into overseas markets. The client list included an impressive number of blue chip customers, including British Airways, Austin Rover, J. Sainsbury and British Telecom.

Suddenly shaking free of corporate restraints has a major impact on the team's motivation and enthusiasm. The freedom to manoeuvre, to make key decisions and to see their direct consequences, is an exciting, sometimes even intoxicating, experience. If this is communicated fully to the rest of the workforce, it can have a cascading effect throughout the company.

But can this enthusiasm be communicated to the workforce? That will largely depend on how the managers market the buyout. If they and the vendor want the buyout to take place with the minimum of fuss, they may keep employees in the dark until everything is tied up. In our survey, a handful of management teams had kept the buyout a total secret and reported that, to this day, their employees still do not know about the change in ownership.

In general, telling the workforce about the buyout – immediately and directly – can have considerable advantages. It can be a unique opportunity for top management to inform employees about how the business is performing and to generate greater involvement and commitment.

In the case of Premier Brands, Judge and the other directors made strenuous efforts to inform the workforce about the buyout and to spell out the company's new financial position. The management buyout was well received by the employees and was seen as a much preferable option to being taken over. The management team undertook innumerable personal presentations to the employees and made good use of internal publications. Employees were told candidly that the company's borrowing levels were now based on its own financial standing, instead of the huge capacity of the parent company.

'We know that if the banks don't like what they see, they will take their money away. There is no margin for error', Martin Bralsford, the finance director, told the workforce at the time of the buyout. The team clearly spelt out the high price of independence. Employees were told that interest on the money borrowed to finance the buyout cost £1,000 an hour, a figure which emphasized the need for the tightest control on financial policies. While the constraints of being within a large company had been removed, the new managers emphasized that new pressures now operated. 'The buck stops with us now', Judge told the company. 'We can't turn to "Big Brother" to bail us out. We know that we have only one chance to make our company work.'

A large part of this communications effort may be directed towards reassuring employees about the future of the company and that their employment conditions will not be affected adversely by the buyout. The buyout team's relationship with the trade unions is important here; it must make sure that it does not underestimate the reaction of the union representatives. Most unions will be suspicious of the buyout as they fear that large-scale redundancies often follow. This suspicion is lessening, however, as increasing numbers of buyouts involve profitable subsidiaries, instead of badly performing businesses.

The Nicholas Mendes study found that employees and trade unions generally reacted favourably to the buyout, although the management team's initial announcement provoked widespread concern over job security. In the eyes of the management team, white collar/blue collar relations had improved considerably after the buyout, with employees demonstrating greater loyalty and commitment.

Coyne and Wright's study revealed that management buyouts are neither more nor less likely to experience trade union problems or industrial action than in other comparable companies. Even in the cases when job losses were involved, trade union resistance was minimal; out of the 49 companies issuing redundancies, 41 reported no action from the unions, eight reported slight resistance and only two companies said strong actions had been taken. In most of the companies surveyed, industrial relations had actually improved after the buyout, and employees' motivation, morale and involvement had considerably strengthened.

If industrial relations problems do arise, the solution is generally for the team to persevere and to reassure employees that the buyout is in everyone's interest, as one management team discovered. The chief executive explains:

> We informed our employees about the buyout two weeks before negotiations were concluded. Their initial reaction, which lasted for some time after the buyout, was one of scepticism and that head office was trying to pull the wool over their eyes.

Employees suspected that the buyout had been manipulated because the subsidiary was likely to go into liquidation. If the buyout took place before this happened, the parent company would not have to pay redundancy costs. 'How else could they explain that two other ailing subsidiaries had been closed down and theirs, which had been in a similar position, was being sold off?' asks the executive. 'However, many of these problems settled down as we managed to keep our heads above water.'

(iv) Finance

'The first two years of the buyout are the period of maximum risk', commented Mike Cumming, manager of Barclays Development Capital, to *Your Business*. 'You'll get through this if your market is growing and interest rates are static. But if interest rates suddenly rise, a number of buyouts will be in considerable trouble.'

The first two years after the buyout will be all about control of spending and imposing strict controls on cashflow. Buyout managers will have to resist the temptation to award themselves perks like company cars, as investors are looking for financial probity. Stable growth and consolidation must be key aims, otherwise servicing the buyout debt will become an increasingly heavy weight as the size of repayments grows heavier each year.

Many buyout companies will not experience any problems at all, particularly if they are bought out subsidiaries which were financially independent before the buyout. Research has revealed that companies which have been bought out of receivership and which were already experiencing financial difficulties are more likely to see real problems with cashflow after the buyout. However, it has also been shown that if the structure of the deal takes cashflow difficulties into account, the buyout can be used as a means to refinance the business and inject sufficient cash resources.

One buyout company which had experienced financial problems beforehand found that the buyout had a very positive effect on its relations with bankers and investors. The chief executive comments: 'We were amazed at the amount of goodwill around. There was no problem with finance, which we found to be the most surprising thing of all. In fact, we were offered far more facilities than were really needed. We were able to pick and choose.'

The main problem for bought out companies is to attain the performance targets forecast. If the company finds that it is failing to achieve a good enough rate of growth in the early years, it is frequently a sign that the business is too highly geared. 'There are going to be some bloody noses soon', warns Electra's Roger Brooke. 'Some management teams have been paying some very silly prices for their companies.' The company in these circumstances will find it increasingly difficult to keep up with repayments, most of which are only manageable in the medium term if early growth targets are achieved. It may well be that new financing is eventually needed, which will inevitably lead to a dilution of the team's equity share. As a buyout investor comments:

> The whole reason why we finance a buyout is because the company should have strong profit potential. We follow a hands-off policy for the first three years and let the company settle down. Then we look at it to see if it is reaching its targets and if it needs refinancing.

Another common problem is poor debtor control and financial management. It is for this reason that financial institutions are often unwilling to back buyout companies, which lack strong credit control systems. In the case of bought out subsidiaries, the management may have previously been protected by the parent company from the consequences of its poor financial controls and systems. The managers may find themselves in for a rude awakening after the buyout, especially if it becomes patently obvious that the new finance director is not capable of adjusting to the higher level of financial management.

Conclusion

Successfully completed buyout deals are sometimes looked on as commercial panaceas. After a blaze of publicity, excitement and enthusiasm, the new team often feels heavily pressurized to produce impressive results overnight. In reality, it has to steer the company through a difficult transition period, as managers and employees adjust to independence and as new management and financial systems are introduced. Whatever happens, this new freedom and independence does not come cheaply. While there are undoubtedly a number of outstanding successes, most buyouts achieve only moderate growth and profits. And, for a small number of buyout teams, the price of freedom will be too high.

No two buyouts are ever the same; some buyouts will be completed simply and easily while others will take months of protracted and tortuous negotiating. Buyout managers will experience different problems and must rely to a large extent on their own abilities and ingenuity to find the solutions. Indeed, the ability to steer a path through the buyout minefield is one of the qualifications for obtaining the backing the buyout team seeks. In the following pages we tap into this wealth of knowledge by describing the experiences of 13 buyout companies operating in widely diverse industries. Each case study provides many rich insights into the complexities of achieving and managing a buyout. Together they shed considerable light on the ups and downs of becoming an owner/manager. It is a tough, but by no means unrewarding, task.

7

Parker Pen – The Buyout as an International Turn-around Mechanism

After five years of inner turmoil, leadership problems and sliding market shares, the US-owned Parker Pen put itself up for sale. Lulled into a false sense of security by its global presence and quality reputation, the world's largest quality pen producer had slipped slowly into a financial crisis. Its resources were being sapped by heavy losses in the US market, where the company had lost a sizeable portion of its market share. By the early 1980s, Parker was clearly in serious trouble.

But some parts of the group were still showing strong returns. In particular, the European operation, based in Sussex and headed by Jacques Margry, had long been the company's most profitable section. In Britain, Parker had more than a 50 per cent share of the quality pen market. Frustrated and largely helpless to influence the American leadership, Margry and his senior directors were convinced that the group was making some serious strategic errors.

The British management believed that many of the problems in the US stemmed from a damaging marketing strategy, which had taken Parker away from its traditional market niche in high quality pens.

By 1985, the group owned only 17 per cent of the US quality market for pens costing over $3, and a 3 per cent share in the total US writing instruments industry. It had increasingly lost ground to its major competitor, A.T. Cross, which held some 50 per cent of the market for quality pens and 11 per cent of the overall market.

The decline in sales was largely due to the company's move in the early 1980s down-market to produce pens costing less than $3, where 60 per cent of the industry's trade occurred. In doing so, Parker pitted itself against giants such as BIC, which virtually held a stranglehold on disposable pens. It soon found itself losing the fight, mainly because it had underestimated the difficulties of penetrating the bottom end of the market and failed to adapt its marketing and production techniques. The costly and time-consuming experiment only damaged the company's high quality image and moved it away from its traditional strengths in quality production and development.

Much of the loss of direction arose because of leadership problems. For five years, the company had gone through a number of chief executives, almost all of whom had unsuccessfully attempted to steer the company in a new direction.

In January 1982, James Peterson, a marketing man who cut his teeth with tobacco giant R. J. Reynolds and the US Pillsbury food and catering company, succeeded George Parker, grandson of the founder. Peterson immediately centralized the company in an attempt to make it more competitive and market-driven. He cut the workforce savagely, reducing the number of employees from 6,800 to around 3,400. He reduced the product range by 80 per cent to 100 lines and injected $20 million into modernizing production facilities.

Peterson was particularly concerned with raising Parker's market share. He did this through lowering prices, to the extent that, two years later, Parker had the largest share in six of the ten biggest markets in the world. But in such a labour-intensive company, Peterson's price cuts proved too severe. Labour costs soared, while earnings continued to fall.

Peterson's successor Mitchell Fromstein, who heads Parker's manpower temporary help business which was part of the group until the buyout, spoke to *International Management* about that stage of Parker's history. He commented:

There had to be a cost reduction and refinancing. Losses were such that debt had been built up. That, plus the cost of capital, plus debt interest, plus corporate headquarters cost, was eating up the profit.

In Margry's view, Peterson's measures were necessary but not enough to turn the group around. He commented to *International Management:*

Peterson came in to do a number of things under the same owners and was therefore under some restrictions. As an outsider, he couldn't do what we can do and was forced to compromise.

Peterson's decision to take Parker down-market caused deep division in the company. His second major decision – to fire Parker's 40 advertising agencies around the world and use the US multinational agency Ogilvy and Mather – was just as unpopular. Peterson's commitment to global marketing resulted in his aim to have a single advertising strategy, with advertisements which could be used worldwide. His approach was considered by many to be too crude for a market that was both diverse and mature in terms of appeal and competition.

Peterson resigned and was replaced by Fromstein in January 1985. He decided to concentrate on the company's strong tradition for quality production and withdrew the company from the disposable pen market.

It quickly became clear to Fromstein and the Parker family that the company, which was now in better shape, needed restructuring and a totally new style of leadership. The US manpower temporary help business, headed by Fromstein, had never really fitted into the group and would clearly benefit from being an autonomous business. Currency translation was another important consideration as 75 per cent of Parker's sales occurred outside the US. When the dollar was weak during the 1970s, strong foreign sales were converted into large dollar profits. But the strengthening of the dollar since the beginning of the 1980s had exposed Parker to currency translation losses. The company would plainly reap considerable benefit from being located outside the US.

The US owners also realized that the company needed a more entrepreneurial style of leadership. 'The initial turnaround steps have been taken. The company is now producing a profit, but what's needed is for a tight management team which has been running the successful side of the business to put some of their own assets at risk and take an entrepreneurial approach', Fromstein commented when the sale of the company was announced in July 1985.

The decision caused great excitement among the European management. It dawned upon Margry and his colleagues that they had the long awaited opportunity to release the European division from the restraints of Parker's large centralized structure.

'The idea for a buyout never originated from one person; it just slowly evolved over the months prior to the announcement to sell', recalls Robert Barnsley, group finance director. 'We disagreed with the way that the company was being run, but our views fell on stony ground. we had discussed a buyout casually with each other, but we never seriously thought it could ever happen. Then the company went up for sale and we thought, "Why not?" '

Loyalty to Parker was a main reason why the idea of a buyout was nothing more than a lunchtime topic among the European management for so many months. Several of the managers felt that a buyout was an act of betrayal, but the decision to sell Parker allowed them to cast their doubts aside. 'Once we got over the psychological barrier of being seen as disloyal, we suddenly realized that buyout was a reality', comments James Moller, group secretary.

As yet, the possibility of buying the entire company had not even entered the minds of the buyout team. Buying the European operations was one thing; buying a group which sprawled over several continents, traded in 150 different countries and produced writing instruments with an annual retail sales value of £115 million, seemed an impossible task altogether.

Suddenly, the management team was plunged into a hectic race to produce a bid before Parker's trade competitors. Within weeks of the announcement to sell, giants like Dunhill and Gillette were prowling around; there was even a rumour that Pilot, the Japanese company, was considering making a bid.

It seemed natural that Margry, who had thirty years of experience with Parker, should head the buyout. All the directors recognized the clarity and flair of his vision for the company and his unrivalled grasp of the industry. A number of the team later said that the eventual success of the buyout was largely due to his credibility with the selling company and financial institutions alike.

Ignoring the question of whether he would be able to raise the necessary finance for the buyout, Margry set out to form the team. In his eyes, pinpointing the right individuals was the most crucial task of all. 'If you have the best team in town, it greatly increases your chances of winning whatever game you play', he comments. Margry carefully selected an initial group of six directors, picked from different management teams around the world. These key individuals were eventually to become the new company's executive directors. 'I wrote and asked them if they were prepared to mortgage themselves up to the hilt and work 12–14 hours a day', he recalls.

The broad structure of the buyout began to take shape when Margry met a contact from advisers, Cockman, Copeman and Partners. They suggested that Schroder Venture, with its international experience, would be the most suitable financial institution. Taking with him three-year projections and cashflow predictions, and having little idea of what to expect, Margry met Schroder's Jon Moulton. While the company's response was positive, it immediately advised Margry to inform the Parker family of the plan for a buyout.

Within days of talking with the Parker family in the US, the scale of the buyout was drastically enlarged. The Parker family, not wishing to see the company absorbed by a trade competitor, gave cautious approval to the team, but only on the stipulation that the buyout should include the entire company.

Buying the multinational company seemed an impossible task. The team's first response was to consider selling off sections of the company through a series of secondary buyouts to the national managements of the Asia/Pacific and Latin American sections, 'but it was simply too complex to both buy and sell simultaneously', comments Barnsley. Splitting up the company raised other problems. Almost all of the the buyout team were committed to remaining as a single company. Also, most of the manufacturing business was based at the UK headquarters in Newhaven, Sussex, making localized buyouts unfeasible.

But the most important consideration of all was protecting the Parker brand name. Margry and his team realized that the company's reputation for quality was its most valuable asset. Barnsely comments: 'Lose that, and we damage the business beyond repair. We had to buy the entire company if we were to control quality levels and protect our brand name'.

As Margry and his team reassessed their position, they began to question their assumption that it would be impossible to buy the entire company. Their confidence was fuelled by the fact that they were sitting on the most profitable part of the company. The European division was, after all, producing 65 per cent of the worldwide profits and 55 per cent of the sales. 'We had become a market leader in Europe; why couldn't we do the same thing in the US and the other countries?' asks Moller.

It was not surprising that the team was initially so cautious about buying the entire company. The poor performance of the US division – it had made losses of more than $5 million during 1985 – could prove a disastrous liability to the new company. Drastic measures needed to be taken to bring the division back to prosperity. Just as importantly, the financial institutions had to be convinced that it could be done. Should the buyout go ahead, the US losses would have to be stemmed immediately, putting the spotlight straight away on Margry's leadership. 'The US business was a make or break situation. We had about six weeks to find a way of stopping it being such a drag on the business', Barnsley comments.

Bankers Trust, Electra Investment Trust and Chemical Venture Capital were interested in financing the deal. In their eyes, the company had several strengths, including a long established brand name; a strong presence in world markets; a good product range; a long relationship with retailers; and considerable experience selling up-market.

The financial investors were opposed to retaining the US division, which consisted of a large production plant, a large distribution centre and the costly headquarters in Janesville, Wisconsin. But, by then, the management team believed that it was essential to retain a foothold in the massive US market. Should they close down the US production plants, the capacity of the modernized manufacturing plant at Newhaven would be insufficient to serve the US market, especially if Parker's sales increased. Whatever happened, the major production plants around Janesville would have to be retained.

Besides gaining the support of the financial institutions, the buyout team had to convince the Parker family of the feasibility of its plans. 'There was at least one serious contender which the Parker family knew could provide the $100 million for the company. The family was less certain of our ability.' This meant that the team had to draw up detailed plans of how it would restore the company's profitability, rationalize its structure and cut costs. It would also have to formulate an aggressive and convincing marketing strategy that would ensure that Parker regained its market share worldwide.

'The most crucial decision we made during that time was how to spread our production throughout our plants located in the US, Newhaven, Paris and in South and Central America', says Barnsley. The management team calculated that the £6 million modernization programme at Newhaven had made production costs there as cheap as in the US. It was decided that the US plants would cater for the US market alone. The UK plant would service Europe and Asia/Pacific.

The team decided to scrap the research and development department, which had been centralized and relocated in the US since the early 1980s. Although it cost £3 million a year to run, the management team felt that it had seen no tangible benefit from the department. Eventually, the management team estimated that it could reduce the US workforce to a minimum of 450.

Margry had no doubts about the marketing strategy for the US division. He planned to move the business immediately up-market, through a mixture of product development, packaging and advertising. The company would become more visible in the retail sector and build on a nostalgic awareness of Parker Pen. Although A.T. Cross dominated the market, it was Parker's only serious competitor, with a product range which Margry and the other directors believed was old and limited. 'By mid-November 1985, we knew we could make the US business viable', says Moller.

Throughout October and November 1985, the management team feverishly gathered the data for its buyout proposal. Barnsley comments:

> We were totally unprepared for the detailed information that was needed. It was a huge task gathering financial information about such a dispersed group. We had access to only a limited volume of records. Our knowledge about the other world divisions was quite scanty because most of

> the marketing and financial detail was held in the US headquarters, which was naturally not over anxious to help us.

It soon discovered that the operation needed a multi-disciplined approach, which made it essential for the whole team to keep closely in touch. 'From a practical point of view, God knows what we would have done if the facsimile hadn't been invented', comments Moller. The intense pressure never eased off during the six months of the buyout: 'Some of the excitement starts to wear off', admits Moller.

Well aware that many buyouts fail because of the unrealistic optimism of the buyout team, the Parker Pen directors decided to err on the side of caution. 'We spoke as one voice. Not one of us felt we ought to be over optimistic in any area', says Barnsley. Their sales predictions were almost severely cautious. Because so little was known about the Latin American section, zero growth was predicted; even in Europe, where the market penetration was very high, growth was estimated at 2–3 per cent only.

The tremendous pressure on the buyout had a knock-on effect on the rest of the European operation. Much of the day-to-day running of the company had to be left to middle and senior managers, many of whom felt, the directors now admit, forgotten and uninvolved. A number of the team had to fly to the US several times to gather information, which made the process even more time-consuming. 'It became incredibly hectic during the deal', comments Moller. 'In retrospect, we underestimated the amount of time it would take and the strain on our private lives. We all used to joke that we were potential divorcees.'

Relations with the US operations were strained throughout the buyout. Large-scale redundancies were unavoidable if the US operation was going to be saved, and although the Parker family and Fromstein supported the buyout, many of the US staff were hostile and uncooperative. There was also a sizeable lobby against the buyout from the trade unions and the Janesville community. The buyout also attracted somewhat hostile attention from the media. The buyout team embarked upon a delicate public relations exercise, focusing on the message that it wanted to save as many jobs as possible in the US. Moller comments:

> The uncertainty about the buyout was natural in such a small farming town as Janesville. Parker had been established in the US for 100 years

> and many people in Janesville had grown up believing the company was an integral part of the US and particularly a Janesville institution.

Part of the oppostion from the media stemmed from the fact that control of Parker was passing into the hands of a foreign company, 'but as the results of the trading position of the US operation were made public, it became clear that something had to be done', says Barnsely. 'Eventually the media and the trade unions accepted the reality of the situation.'

The final packaging of the deal was, in the event, the easiest aspect of the whole buyout. By the end of December 1985, a sum of $100 million had to be found from the financial institutions and the Parker family. Some $70 million would go to the old family, with $60 million paid almost instantly and a further $10 million later when various legal and financial matters had been settled in France, Canada and Australia. An additional $30 million would be loaned to Parker, either to arrange refinancing or to guarantee borrowing facilities.

Parker was satisfied with the level of gearing. In Barnsley's words:

> The most important aspects about arranging a buyout is to know your company. You must have an intimate knowledge of the business to get the right level of gearing. You have to be confident that you can repay the debt quickly. If you lack those two things, you're heading for trouble.

Of the £71 million that was paid by Parker's investors, £11 million was converted into shares in the company, £15 million into a loan arrangement and a further sum of £45 million was made available by Bankers Trust. Some £300,000 worth of shares were reserved for the seven new executives and a further 13 managers. 'These people put their own money on the table', says Margry. 'That demands sacrifice; it hurts.'

Reshaping the company for future growth

The results of Parker Pen's first six months of trading since the buyout were remarkable. Under the former US owners, the company made losses of around £300,000 in 1985. Under the new management, pre-tax profits reached £3.64 million between March and August 1986, more than double the amount forecast in the buyout plan.

Sales also turned out higher than predicted. Despite currency weaknesses in key markets and a fluctuating dollar, sales were £55.3 million, a rise of 6 per cent over the expected £52.3 million. Much of this increase stemmed from distributors' renewed confidence in the company's stability and future. During the buyout negotiations, severe stock reductions were made as distributors waited to see if competitors such as Dunhill and Gillette would gain control of Parker Pen. Such an outcome could seriously undermine their relationship with the company, especially if significant rationalization took place. In the event, most major distributors took a financial stake in the buyout through taking first convertible cumulative redeemable preference shares.

The company's poor performance in the US market was the first knotty problem which Margry and his team had to tackle. During 1985, the US operation lost more than $5 million: under the new ownership these losses were transformed to a first-half profit of $600,000. Besides moving up-market again, with a resulting sales increase of 12 per cent, the annual costs of the US operations were sharply cut by selling the prestigious headquarters. The workforce was cut by half, bringing the total number of employees to about 440. In total, annual costs were cut by around $20 million in six months.

On a global scale, Parker Pen took some significant steps towards realizing its vision for future health and growth. Sales in Brazil and Argentina rose by more than 50 per cent during the first half of 1986, with dividends worth £1 million issued from Latin America, compared to only £250,000 over the last 20 years. The company's position in the Far East has been further strengthened by the appointment of a new distributor in Taiwan, while further inroads into the lucrative French market have been made.

Developing new market niches

Now Parker Pen is reassessing its range of products and searching for new markets. It is concentrating all its efforts into strengthening its up-market image by developing a limited range of quality, highly priced pens. The company's product range had already been reduced from 500 to 100. Margry is convinced that the time is ripe to develop a single product which can be marketed globally. 'We aim to speak to the market in its own language', he says. He envisages a basic design, with a finish that appeals to different national or cultural tastes, ranging from ornate or gold finished products for Asia and Latin America, for example, to plainer finishes for the Anglo-Saxon markets.

Existing products are also being constantly refined, in keeping with the company's strong tradition of product development. 'Building a better pen', the slogan of the founder, George Parker, still forms the basis of a carefully considered research and development strategy. George Parker consistently introduced new pen designs, patenting the first slip-on pen cap, for example, and the first jointless pen, which solved the problem of leaking ink. Throughout its 100-year history, the company has increased its market share mainly by refining its products. Now Margry is intent on adding new finishes to Parker's product range, as well as developing designer pens.

The new management team has decided that it will set prices, and take overall control of design, research and development, product range and packaging. It is committed to a policy of decentralization for all other key functions, leaving the choice of marketing strategy to local heads. Each division has a different slice of the market and competes against a different rival; Parker Pen faces Sheaffer in Britain; Waterman in France; the Dunhill-owned Mont Blanc in West Germany; and A. T. Cross and Sheaffer in the US.

Says Barnsley: 'Parker has become a listening company. We encourage local general managers to develop their own market and convince us of their market need.'

Future success

The basic building blocks of the company now seem to be in place. The strong and experienced leadership at Parker Pen has concentrated on two major areas: formulating a clear and simple global strategy and developing an organizational structure in which this can take place.

This is well on the way to being achieved: production lines have been rationalized; overheads and costs drastically reduced; the workforce trimmed down; and the management hierarchy streamlined. A consistent marketing strategy has been formulated, centring on Parker Pen's strong brand name and reputation for quality. The worldwide company now has a structure of decentralized, semi-autonomous units which, it hopes, will allow a new degree of market responsiveness and innovation.

The next stage of the company's development is already being considered by the board. A stock exchange listing is a key priority, but the company knows it has first to establish a solid track record as well as a strong financial base. Another issue is beginning to surface. A number of the directors and senior managers are in their late fifties and already Margry is starting to concentrate on succession planning. He and the other directors are well aware that if the company is to be successfully floated, it has to convince the market that its stability will not be undermined by leadership problems. And after such intense efforts to buy Parker Pen, it is unlikely that they will leave the future of the company to chance.

As Margry said to his new management team when it took over: 'We must stop playing games. This is a new company with just one chance to succeed.'

8

Haden – The Buyout as a Takeover Defence Mechanism

Trafalgar House's bid for Haden plc came unannounced on 20 February 1984. 'It was unwanted and undiscussed', recalls Haden's chairman, Peter Simonis.

> They just rang up the managing director one night at 7:30 and asked if we could meet Nigel Broackes next morning. We had seen a little buying of our shares that indicated a bid might be in the offing. So we said yes. They slapped a bid on the table and said they hoped it could be an amicable agreement. I said this was not possible, there had been no prior discussion to even consider. It was too low and had no advantages for Haden. We'd fight and may the best man win. They said they understood.

It was a pretty short discussion.

> We had met in the boardroom upstairs. As Broackes was going out he stopped and looked at a picture of the battle of Trafalgar we had in the room. He said to Eric Parker that the signal was wrong. Parker said it was right. I said 'We put it there for your benefit; look at it well' – to which Philip Ling added 'We hope you won't see it again'.

Trafalgar's bid was highly opportunistic. Haden, having had a couple of tough years, had put its house in order and was set for rapid gains in growth and profits. Trafalgar recognized that it might be able to acquire an undervalued asset cheaply.

Haden's business lay in three main areas: building, industrial and process engineering; industrial finishing and mechanical handling; and specialist engineering. All three had hit a severe recession and profits had been dented by weak trading conditions, with the company dipping into loss in the first half of 1984. In particular, it had been hit by problems with contracts in the Middle East.

But Haden had certainly not been complacent about its performance. As the company reported in the circulars it sent to shareholders advising them not to accept the Trafalgar bid:

Haden's profits grew in each year over the period 1978–1982, from £2.7 million to £8.6 million. However, the fall in profits in 1983 and the first half of 1984 caused the Board to initiate a vigorous and radical reorganization of the Group's activities, including the appointment to Mr. P.H. Ling as the new Group Managing Director. We have sold or closed, or are in the process of so doing, those loss-making businesses with no prospect of an early return to satisfactory profitability. Our continuing businesses are being made more autonomous and accountable.

The principal measures taken (for which full provision has been made in the 1984 accounts) have been the following:

– the French industrial finishing factory and mechanical handling activity have been closed

– negotiations for the sale of the French and Belgian air conditioning and after-sales businesses are under way

– redundancy programmes have been implemented in the contintental industrial finishing units reducing them to satellite status, with back-up service provided from the UK

– the Haden Drysys operating company in Germany has been merged with a successful German partner, Haden retaining a 60 per cent shareholding

– the UK industrial finishing research and development department has been integrated within the expanded research and development unit in the United States

– certain of the specialist engineering companies, notably Haden Food Machinery and Haden Industrial Engineering have been closed.

New Managing Directors have been appointed to Haden Drysys UK, Haden Drysys Belgium, Haden Moore Engineering, Gregson Pipework and Haden Maintenance.

A major element of the losses attributable to discontinued businesses and the extraordinary losses of the last two years has been our activities in France and, to a lesser extent, in Belgium. The rationalization and restructuring in these countries have been particularly far-reaching with the numbers employed in France reducing to no more than 40 personnel, compared with 300 a year ago. In Belgium the numbers employed will be down to around 20.

'By the time the bid came, our profits were moving up again. But a bad year had depressed our share price', says Simonis. From a high of nearly 300 in 1983, it had dropped as low as 130. When Trafalgar began to buy shares, the price had recovered somewhat to 184 and by the time the bid was announced, the price had reached 232.

Trafalgar offered 240 and justified its offer on two grounds – the recent poor performance of the company and the potential for synergy within the Trafalgar Group. Among its comments on performance were the following:

Our Offer of 240p cash per Haden Share is made against the background of Haden's declining financial performance and strategic errors both in acquisitions and geographical diversification. This has culminated in the last two years in a major closure and reorganizational programme which has had a dramatic adverse effect on the net worth of Haden.

We expect Haden's results for the full year in 1984 to show a significant decline in operating profit over 1983 reflecting a continuing deterioration in operating margins. Further substantial extraordinary charges in the second half of 1984 for closure and reorganization costs were forecast by your Chairman in the Interim Statement issued on 27th September, 1984. As a result the net worth of your company may have declined to little more than £20 million (equivalent to 130p per share).

Since 1982, the year when Haden's profits reached a peak, the dividends for Ordinary Shareholders have remained static at the 1982 level of 8.625p (net) per share. In 1983 this dividend was barely covered by the available profits. In 1984 your Board declared a maintained interim dividend of 2.25p (net) costing in total some £349,000. This would have been paid entirely out of reserves, attributable losses having totalled £2,817,000.

Notwithstanding your Chairman's recognition that further extraordinary costs would be incurred in the second half of 1984, he stated in the Interim Statement for 1984 that 'Based on current operating performance, it is the Board's intention to maintain the final 1984 dividend at the same level as 1983.' It seems that this final dividend, costing almost £1 million, will also be paid out of your company's reserves, leading to a further decline in the net worth of your business.

Against this background, it is hardly surprising that the performance of your shares in the last three years has been disappointing. The graph below illustrates the share price movement in the three years prior to our first purchase of Haden Shares on 28th December, 1984 and also highlights its significant under-performance relative to the FTA-A11 Share Index.

In effect, Trafalgar was suggesting that the company was overtrading.

Trafalgar explained the opportunities for synergy between the two businesses in these terms:

Haden is a market leader in the specialist contracting markets in which it operates. Its businesses in the Building, Industrial and Process Engineering Division and the Specialist Engineering and Contracting Division are complementary, both in terms of specialist expertise and geographical spread, to Trafalgar's existing mechanical and electrical engineering businesses operated through Young, Austen & Young, Rashleigh Phipps Electrical and RDL Electrical-Mechanical Services. The combined group would offer a comprehensive building services capability to clients both in the United Kingdom and overseas, whilst at the same time each operating company would market and develop its own particular products and expertise.

Industrial finishing and mechanical handling are not areas in which Trafalgar is presently involved. Trafalgar will review these activities of Haden closely on acquisition in order to determine how best to maximise their potential.

In particular, Trafalgar saw opportunities to involve Haden in developments in the North Sea.

The Haden board turned for help to its merchant bank, J. Henry Schroder Wagg. Simonis recounts:

> We started by doing a conventional defence. We had a good case to defend – a good balance sheet; money in the bank (some £12 million), no gearing; and a good order book. We were in a good position to defend ourselves.

Trafalgar took its time to send out the offer document and meanwhile the share price climbed steadily. Schroder and the Haden board beavered away to prepare the draft defence documents in readiness. They pointed out that the reorganization had been successfully accomplished and that it was on target for a rapid expansion of both turnover and profits. The share price was now at around 300, so the Trafalgar bid represented a massive discount. Haden also attacked the logic of the fit between the two companies, explaining:

> Haden disagrees fundamentally with Trafalgar House's assertion that

> the building, industrial and process engineering businesses of Haden will benefit from association with Trafalgar House. It is our strong conviction that the Haden Young business would be seriously and adversely affected by association with Trafalgar House.
>
> The key to Haden Young's success in securing the large contracts which are its speciality has been its independence from main contractors and property developers. This company has therefore been acceptable to and trusted by all parties in the construction industry in working together in the confidential formative stages of contract negotiations. During the five years 1980–84 60 per cent of all orders placed with Haden Young came from a small number of main contractors. These contractors are competitors of Trafalgar House, and if Haden Young were to be owned by a contractor or a property developer (such as Trafalgar House) it would cease to be acceptable to many of its most valued customers, and would wither.
>
> Apart from this loss of business which would result from association with Trafalgar House, Haden sees no significant gain from such an association. It is to be assumed that any building services business (including business in the North Sea) which it is in a position to award internally is already placed with its existing subsidiaries, Young, Austen & Young, Rashleigh Phipps and RDL Electrical-Mechanical Services. In consequence, there could be no additional business available to Haden Young.

In the case of the Industrial Finishing and Mechanical Handling Division, Trafalgar House's comment – under the heading 'Complementary businesses' – is as follows:

> Industrial finishing and mechanical handling are not areas in which Trafalgar is presently involved. Trafalgar will review these activities of Haden closely on acquisition in order to determine how best to maximize their potential.
>
> In short, Trafalgar House has made its bid with no specialist knowledge and no clear plans in mind for a part of the Haden business which contributed a turnover of over £100 million in 1984 and which is expected to be a major contributor to the Haden Group results in 1985.

'They fundamentally misunderstood our business', recalls Simonis. 'Building engineering services – they understood that. But automation and industrial finishing systems, they didn't understand at all. They thought the largest part of our profits was in the building engineering services area, when in reality 60 per cent of our turnover and profit were in the other areas.'

It seemed a good case, but Simonis was concerned that it might not be good enough. He recalls:

> We were 10 days into this affair, and I said to my in-house team that a much higher price was certain to emerge. But on the conventional route, it was my feeling that if they were determined to get us, they would because they were big enough and strong enough. *Unless* we could pull another trick out of the hat. Everyone agreed. So the idea of a management buyout was born. I just asked Schroder, could we do it? I didn't know the mechanics.

Schroder brought in its venture capital arm, Schroder Ventures, who evaluated the potential for a buyout. Haden, it quickly discovered, did not fit the normal profile of a buyout candidate in all respects. As Schroder's N.R. Macandrew, who advised the company, explains:

> A typical MBO candidate has a strong asset base, a strong balance sheet, good and reliable cashflow and a vigorous management. Most important of all, however, is the price. What made an MBO particularly possible for Haden was the exit prospective price earnings ratio of 9. This might seem ridiculously low for a p/e ratio in a takeover but, given that the historic exit p/e was over 80, there was a degree of not insubstantial risk associated with the buyout.
>
> Haden did have a strong balance sheet, but it did not have a particularly strong asset base. On the other hand as a contractor, it did not need to. Its principal assets were current rather than fixed. I had always thought that high asset cover was essential to any MBO but it is not absolutely so. In Haden's case, the net asset cover was small. By comparison, however, the gross asset cover was large as it had over £400 million of work-in-progress, debtors and other assets.

As regards cashflow, Haden's projections indicated that it was about to enter a three-year period of rapid cash generation. If it had been a cash-consuming business, it would have been a non-starter as far as an MBO was concerned.

Since Trafalgar had taken its time to bring out the offer document, Schroder advised Haden to take its time in responding. The overt and the covert defences would have to run in parallel. It was, Simonis remembers, a time-consuming business, helped by the fact that, according to Macandrew:

> We had a board which was eminently advisable. Instead of rushing about in all directions like a chicken with its head cut off (like some boards in takeovers), it stayed very much together, was a willing listener and

taker of advice, was a vigorous defender of its independence and, most importantly, was willing to be adventurous and positive.

To make the bid, Simonis and his colleagues acquired an off-the-shelf company, Manugood Ltd. Schroder meanwhile began to put together the kind of capital structure that the new company would need. In the end, the bank and the Haden directors agreed on a package that consisted of £500,000 of ordinary capital, £500,000 of redeemable ordinary shares, £19 million of redeemable preference capital and £37 million of debt. The debt comprised some £27 million of fixed term facilities and £10 million of temporary facilities, which could be paid back from the £10 million Haden had in the kitty.

'The £19 million of redeemable preference shares (known as mezzanine finance) was created to rank behind the borrowings but in front of the equity', says Macandrew. 'As such, its cost to Manugood was rather high but it was an essential ingredient of the total package.'

The equity package of £1 million was split equally between straightforward and redeemable ordinary shares. The reason the equity was kept so small was to accommodate the management of Haden as their involvement was absolutely essential. Their own financial capability was therefore relevant. It was judged that they should be entitled to 15 per cent of the equity as a minimum (requiring them to subscribe £150,000). Moreover, to incentivize them, it was judged that this percentage should be capable of rising to 30 per cent if certain profit or cashflow criteria were met – hence the redeemable ordinary shares (none of which were subscribed by management) which, if redeemed, would give management not £150,000 out of £1 million (or 15 per cent) but £150,000 out of £500,000 (or 30 per cent).

Now the difficult part began. 'Putting together a sales document with a clear, professional, short and easy-to-read business plan was critical', say Simonis. 'Without that, no-one will back you.' But gaining commitment from financial institutions turned out to be something of a Catch–22 exercise. Potential providers of venture capital for the acquisition held off until they saw who was going to provide the debt financing. And the banks approached for debt financing insisted on a prior commitment from the venture capital houses.

This seesaw would have been bad enough had it been an ordinary buyout, but Haden had two other major problems. First was the novelty of using a buyout as a takeover defence. Did the institutions want to get into such a situation? Second was the time pressure.

Under Stock Exchange rules, the victim of a takeover bid has 39 days from the formal bid announcement, in which to put forward a defence. The predator then has an extra few days to make his final pitch. Simonis and his colleagues would have to make their bid before the 39 days were up.

Two key funds – Globe & Electra – agreed to come in. 'Once it was known that Electra was leading the buyout, then a lot of others came in behind them, on the basis that "If it was good for Electra it must be O.K. for us" ', says Simonis.

'Schroder soon found the equity and mezzanine finance backers', recalls Macandrew, but since these things are never allowed to be simple, one major institution was located in the UK and another in the US. Moreover, one wanted lots of equity and not too much mezzanine finance and the other wanted the reverse. The package therefore had to be split. There ensued countless transatlantic telephone calls and plane trips (the stuff of which contested takeovers are made), while the finer details of the participations were worked out in detail. At the same time, equity participations were offered to a small number of supporting institutions because management buyouts are generally arranged on a syndicated basis with reciprocity of opportunity ensuring that the main players get to see most of the principal buyouts. Also the Haden top management allocated the 15 per cent available to it amongst about 25 employees ranging from the executive chairman to divisional heads. This was an unusally large number of participants but it served two valuable purposes. First, it reinforced the loyalty of key employees to Haden and the common cause of making money. Secondly, it must have influenced Trafalgar House against bidding again as it would have judged that depriving the key employees of an opportunity to make money would have potentially soured relationships with the very people on whom it would depend if it was successful in buying Haden.

> We located the equity and mezzanine providers without too much difficulty but I cannot say the same for the bank finance. We decided early on that an American bank would be the best bet because the US banking system is so much more used to MBOs, particularly in a bid situation. We offered the package to three banks initially. Two quickly opted out – so saving both our time and theirs – but the third showed great interest and wheeled in a strong team to conduct the necessary due diligence procedure. Alas, it was not possible to convince this

particular bank of the merits of the transaction and their interest eventually collapsed. It had been sustained during some difficult and protracted negotiations by the enthusiastic and able members of the bank's buyout team but the team leader – the decision maker – could not generate the necessary commitment and the transaction foundered on his doubts. With the benefit of hindsight we should have reacted to his early scepticism by changing horses at that stage; we wasted valuable time and effort on someone who simply was not prepared to come to the party.

We then had two or three other false starts until, late in the day, a large US top quality bank was approached. Its speed of reaction was remarkable. Within just a few days, it had assessed the situation and had written a commitment letter. The particular reasons why they were so quick in their response were firstly their knowledge and experience of MBOs and secondly and more importantly their personal knowledge of key players in the Haden management. This again emphasises the importance which a single person can make to a decision-making process. The mutual trust which had been previously established unlocked the remaining door.

Simonis would have liked to have constructed a package that provided much wider employee ownership. But the need for speed and for secrecy ruled out that particular approach.

The last knots in the financing package were finally tied with no more than 24 hours to go. It was a bombshell to Trafalgar, which had still not raised the terms of its original bid. Trafalgar now demanded that it should be given all the information which the institutions backing the Manugood offer had received. Simonis replied: 'You ask the questions and if we have told the institutions, we'll tell you.'

Having got the answers to its questions, Trafalgar had 21 days to make its own counter-offer. The Haden managers spent several nail-biting weeks as they waited for an announcement. In the end, Trafalgar simply let its bid lapse. Simonis gives two reasons. 'Firstly we were not cheap for them any more. To beat our bid they would have had to pay the full price. The danger was they'd take over an unhappy management. Secondly I think they thought we were paying more than we could handle.'

The institutional shareholders as usual having held off their commitment until the last minute in case someone came in with a late bid, after 21 days the acceptances came in thick and fast. But the tension was far from over. The institutional venture capital investors were insisting on acceptances of 90 per cent from the shareholders. Getting the last 5–10 per cent of acceptances was a major task. Wedges of shares in family trusts have to be identified and the trustees persuaded to sell. Small private shareholders may have moved house and not left a forwarding address.

Trafalgar, which had built up only a small stock, did not come out of the affair empty-handed. Having forced a revaluation of the share price, it was able to sell its block of shares to Manugood at the bid price of 370p – more than doubling its money.

For the Haden management, the deal has been an outstanding success. The debt financing was rapidly repaid, and so, by mid 1987, were the redeemable shareholdings. Now with 30 per cent of the equity, the managers have a great deal of freedom to take the company in the direction they want. Says Simonis:

> The one thing we have is freedom in deciding what we do now. We can refloat on the full market or USM, here or in the USA. We can refinance the company by gearing up again and buying out the institutional shareholders. Or we can sell the company to a good home of our choice.
>
> It was a chance of a lifetime for guys, some of them quite young, to make a bit of money from their efforts.
>
> We have a rather more proprietorial view of the business now. You have a lot more incentive. You don't work any harder. In a company like ours, with a long tradition of loyal people, everyone works hard anyway.

For Schroder, the outcome was not all rosy. True, it had demonstrated a major new takeover defence and enhanced its reputation. But it had lost out financially in that it could not appear to be running with the fox and chasing with the hounds. As Macandrew explains:

> When we eventually raised the matter with the Takeover Panel on a confidential basis about a week or two before any announcement was made, the Panel made a number of requests. Firstly, Schroder or its managed funds could not take an equity interest in Manugood. Secondly, Schroder Ventures could not take a fee from Manugood. Thirdly, we were to give prominence to the role played by Schroder Ventures – we were naturally delighted to comply with that. The first two requirements gave us a problem because we naturally felt that, having constructed the transaction for the benefit of the shareholders, the management and the company itself, it was only fair to be able to participate in the future and to be rewarded for the past. In the

interests, however, of getting the deal done, we complied although we made the point that we were being penalized for doing something that was patently in the interests of shareholders.

Equally critical in this respect was the need to overcome any possible accusation that a bid by Manugood was not high enough. The Manugood bankers initially offered only 350p a share. Schroder calculated 375p and a compromise was reached at 370p. Effectively, this meant that the buyout managers and their bankers had to pay more for the company than would probably have been the case in the absence of a hostile bid.

Macandrew does not see the defensive buyout as a frequent form of response to unwanted bids, but does believe it will become more common. His primary piece of advice for companies which use this device is to ensure that they keep it tightly secret until it is signed and sealed with financial backers, which rules out any possibility of an employee buyout.

> Those who believe that they can air it as a technique and fail to follow through (Debenhams, for example) will be shooting themselves in the foot. We impressed upon Haden throughout that the MBO discussions must not be allowed to leak to the press or the stock market as it would obviously have been damaging to our cause to try to do something and to fail.

Peter Simonis' final comment is: 'It speaks well for our management, advisers and backers that we caught Trafalgar on the wrong foot. Nigel Broackes is a good loser – he had the courtesy to call me and wish us luck.'

9

Roadchef – The Buyout Breaks Up a Troubled Company

It was history repeating itself for Clive Lindley, chairman of the Lindley Catering Investment Group of companies. In 1969, as a director of Banquets of Oxford, he had stood in his chairman's office asking to be allowed a shareholding in the company. When his request was refused, he had quit and set up his own company. Now, although he had enfranchised the chief executives of each of the three companies in the group, Lindley was faced with pressure from an eager middle management in Roadchef, the most successful of the three companies, for a share in the action.

Lindley had established the Roadchef chain of motorway service facilities at a time when the then Ministry of Transport was asking for tenders to operate a range of new sites. The government's aim was to have a complete network of motorway service stations as rapidly as possible. It drove a hard bargain, basing its selection of operators in large part upon who would pay over the greatest percentage of their takings. A travel company, Galleon World Travel Association, was a significant shareholder, and Roadchef was then known as Galleon Roadchef. Its first site, in the Lake District, was on a site acquired by British Petroleum. BP wanted a lessee to handle the catering side of the project and eventually also asked Lindley to manage the petrol sales side under contract.

By 1976, Galleon Roadchef had an additional two sites in Scotland, one at Sandbach in Cheshire, one near Taunton and one near Southampton. But progress in developing them was slow. Along with every other operator, Roadchef found that there was no incentive to invest in improved facilities, when the main beneficiary would be the government rather than the shareholders. Then in 1978 Peter Prior wrote a report for the government on the problems of motorway services, following a flood of criticism in the press. The Galleon shareholders wanted out and Lindley obliged them by buying their equity.

At this stage the LCI Group consisted of Roadchef, with its motorway services, the Midlands-based Lindley Catering Investments, which provided catering services for football fans and Offshore Catering Services, which serviced oil and gas rigs in the North Sea. Lindley ran Roadchef, and while the other two divisional heads served on the Group Board and had shareholdings in the group, they ran their divisions as separate fiefdoms. Also on the board was Patrick Gee, an accountant who had joined the group in 1973. The only function of the group was centralized financial control, which primarily meant moving cash around from one company to another as needed.

By 1980 Lindley's interests were elsewhere, principally with the formation of the Social Democratic Party. A thoroughgoing entrepreneur, it is probably true to say that he was more interested in setting up new ventures than in running them. While not rudderless, the group was suffering from a shortage of cohesion and vision and Gee could see stormclouds gathering. In particular, the Prior report had opened the way to a much more sensible contractual arrangement with the government, but this would require a heavy capital investment programme for which the company was not equipped. The Conservative Government that came in in 1979 was not slow to recognize that it could improve the facilities offered at motorway service stations and extract capital sums from the lessees straightaway, if it renegotiated 50-year leases and scrapped the premium on sales turnover.

Gee persuaded Lindley to allow him to become managing director of the Roadchef division and began a comprehensive programme of restructuring. He slimmed down the management hierarchy and diverted cash saved into modernizing and expanding facilities. But his ability to make the investments needed was hampered by the group financial policy. In effect, Roadchef's profits were supporting the loss-making activities of the other divisions, so Roadchef was cash-starved at a time when it most needed to invest. In 1982, Gee told Lindley bluntly that the group would founder unless some drastic action was taken. Could he buy out the Roadchef division?

Although Lindley agreed in principle, the technicalities of breaking the motorway service operations loose were substantial. The aims of the buyout team – Gee and 30 of his management colleagues – were at variance with Lindley's. He wanted to extract himself from the company with a continuous income and minimal risk; they were happy to take the risks involved in expanding Roadchef, but needed to remove the drain on finances that Lindley's other ventures represented. The answer was to strip out all the reserves from all the subsidiary companies into the holding company. That provided a cash store to meet Lindley's needs and reduced the value of the Roadchef division, which was already highly geared, to a level where it was affordable to the buyout team.

Touring round the venture capital houses in search of a deal to convert borrowings to equity was a depressing experience, recalls Financial Director, Maurice Edgington.

> Their view was that we were getting a good deal out of it, so why worry about their terms and conditions? They wanted everything – an income stream, security for their money, a seat on the board and management fees. They wanted their shares at par, even though management were subscribing at a premium. They were looking to take control if things didn't go well. If it hadn't been for Patrick's creativity and his astute, detailed financial know-how, we might have found ourselves losing all down the line. I don't know what we would have done if Barclays, our clearing bank, had turned us down as well. Of course, now we are successful, the venture capital people fall over themselves to lend us money.

The clearing banks, which already had a strong interest in the company's survival via its borrowings, were eventually convinced that their money would be more secure if the core of the business were spun off. With their backing, Gee formed a new company, in which he retained 70 per cent of the equity and his management colleagues shared 30 per cent. They raised £100,000 between them to buy Roadchef Ltd, debts and all. At the time, in 1983, the company had a sales turnover of £30 million.

The LCI Group, now only two companies, swiftly disintegrated as the managers of Lindley Catering Investments followed Roadchef's lead and arranged their own buyout.

For Gee and his colleagues, the last weeks before the deal was completed were nail-biting. The current managing director Tim Ingram Hill, who joined the company as personnel director in 1979 recalls:

> Our biggest worry was 'Would he sign the paper as agreed?' As he sat there and thought, he had to be thinking: 'Could I do better?' We were also worried that he might sell out to the competition. He'd already spoken to two of them, but couldn't get the price he wanted, because he couldn't pull out the figures for the motorway operations from the rest of the group. We knew if he sold out to anyone but us, we would be out. It was our last throw gamble to survive as a company. Patrick had already left to set up the new company, so we had to force a timetable on Clive. We told him: 'Unless you sign on July 7, it's off.'
>
> When Clive finally signed, when we finally became the owners, we had a feeling of enormous elation. We said: 'Thank God it's over'. Now we can spend the rest of the season running the company our way.

The first issue facing the new owners was how to repay the heavy loans. The predicted upturn in consumer spending arrived, and the fuel price differential disappeared as the oil companies realized that market share was being lost because of high prices on the motorway. The resulting highly positive cashflow during the summer months was used partly to reduce gearing and to invest in improved facilities. (Some of the sites had not even been built on at all, for lack of funds.) By building or refurbishing in the winter, the company was able to demonstrate the commercial viability of each site during the summer, and this in itself did a great deal to assuage the banks' concerns over high gearing.

'Some facilities we bulldozed and started again, to develop the best standards, that would attract people back again. We set the standards the rest of the industry has had to follow', says Ingram Hill. By the end of 1987, all the company's sites will have been refurbished or rebuilt.

Roadchef's nine sites make it the third largest motorway services operator in the UK – behind Trust House Forte and Granada – with around 15 per cent of the total business. Some of the sites it owns itself, others it manages in whole or part. Either way, it has an obligation to provide food and other basic facilities 365 days a year.

Given the opportunity, Gee, who died in 1986, would have liked to have given all employees of the company an equity share. That simply was not possible at the time. 'We had to involve first those people we wanted to motivate first', says Ingram Hill. However, in January 1987, Roadchef became the first company to introduce an Employee Share Ownership Plan (ESOP), under the terms of recent legislation. The owner-managers had been looking for some form of share scheme for employees ever since the buyout, but had never found one that met their needs. Then they were introduced to Unity Trust by George Lawson, National Officer of the Hotel and Catering Workers' Union (part of the giant General Municipal and Boilerworkers' Union), who were looking at the concept of ESOPs in the UK. Ingram Hill explains that it 'allows us to make use of pre-tax profits to offer a potentially tax-free gift of a stake in the company to our employees and at the same time realize some capital for existing shareholders, without going outside the company'.

The ESOP scheme, constructed by Unity Trust, allows any of the 700 employees to receive a free issue of shares after three years service. About one third qualified at the start of the scheme. In the first year, eligible employees received 100 shares for each year of service. Thereafter, they will receive an allocation each year for as long as they remain with the company. The shares are revalued every year, but were worth £2 each at the commencement of the plan. Employees can sell their shares without paying income tax if they retain them for a minimum of five years.

The benefits of the scheme are considerable. It allows the company to raise new capital from within and to involve and motivate the employees; and it provides the shareholders with a ready means of realizing some of their holdings without selling them outside the company and creates an internal market for the shares.

Looking back on the buyout experience, Ingram Hill has the following advice to offer:

- don't be naive when dealing with venture capital firms. Wise up first.
- if you have a good proposition you need never put your house in hock to obtain financial backing.
- do spend time making sure you present your case well. Learn

how to talk the right language. The investors want to know the company will be sensibly controlled by people who know what they are doing.

- make sure there are no unpleasant surprises for the bank or venture capitalists. Tell them about potential problems in a way that shows you know what you are doing and that the risks are minimal.
- don't underestimate the time and effort required to put a successful package together.

10

Bianchi – The Buyout as an Escape From a Merger That Soured

Bianchi Display Group was founded in August 1977 by the managing director Tony Bianchi and a colleague Alan Peach. In those days it was called Alplas Display – a name which had to be changed a year or so later because there was a prior registration. Here Tony Bianchi describes how the buyout came about and how it fared subsequently.

The original objective of the company was to make high-class display cabinets from a modular system with the aim of producing a high-quality, high-value product with a minimal amount of non-skilled or semi-skilled labour. The idea came from a very small operation which had been part of a group of companies which I had worked for previously. But the degree of exploitation amounted merely to showing that a construction system of this kind, if reasonably designed, could be applied to this market, producing a high-quality product at a very low cost.

Although the company struggled in 1977 and the first half of 1978, it finally became involved in supplying purpose-built units for in-store concessions, in both jewellery and cosmetics, in the major department stores. This was a growing market to which the product was ideally suited. By 1979 the company had expanded to a turnover of £300,000 a year with profits just short of £30,000. Among its clients was a successful and rapidly growing jewellery company, which specialized in opening concessions in a wide variety of stores. It wanted to diversify as it was planning to go public the following year. It also felt that our operation would complement its own, not to mention providing it with an in-house source for its display equipment. At the time, the two existing shareholders were extremely tempted by the offer, finding it fairly flattering after such a short time in business. Broadly speaking, there was a cash element of £20,000 together with a share option arrangement in the parent company. (This option was obviously potentially valuable in view of the impending flotation.) In addition, there were fairly generous service contracts.

Part of the idea was that the parent company should provide investment capital to allow the original company to buy other suitable operations which widened its product range and increased its worth as a display company. However, the only thing that happened in the first year was that the parent sourced equipment to re-fit most of its operations at a large discount and did not provide the appropriate working capital to make acquisitions. Very little management time was given to the new subsidiary by the parent, as they were geographically remote and the parent was much too interested in its 'stock flotation' to waste much time on its acquisition. The net result was a loss of about £100,000.

About four months before the flotation, the parent company's managing director approached me, pointing out that the loss would compromise his own profitable situation when it came time to go to the Market. Although the company was in a very bad way – apart from the financial problems, nearly half the company's turnover was now coming from within the group – a package was arranged between the company's creditors, 3i and the Midland Bank to provide sufficient money to mount a rescue operation. The company was purchased back in May 1981 for a nominal sum and the recovery commenced. There were two other directors at this time and it was decided that they would leave as the company could not carry a large board.

The key managers in this situation were the financial controller and the production manager/buyer. Both people performed outstandingly well and the company's situation slowly improved. Very tight cashflow controls were instigated, the creditors were told when they would be paid, and how much of the backlog would be paid off, and this plan was kept to in the vast majority of cases. As the clearing bank was understandably nervous, there were sometimes some very difficult moments to do with the payment of creditors. However, with continued reassurance from the management of the company, credit continued to be extended and very slowly new sales were created. The company returned to profit in 1983. Costs were cut dramatically from £44,000 per month to approximately £27,000 per month, wages were frozen at all levels and an aggressive marketing campaign was undertaken on a shoestring budget.

The main problem encountered was the financial drag of the accrued debt. The interest charges were extremely high and the banks had to be constantly reassured. So much time was spent chasing money and making agreements with creditors that the sales – which should have recovered faster – did not regain their buoyancy for at least a year and a half. However, a profit was made in the financial year 1983–4 and the company has been profitable ever since, expecting to turn in figures of nearly £200,000 in profits on a expected turnover of £2 million during the current financial year.

The management team that effected the turnaround was essentially the same people who were with the company before the takeover (with the exception of the two directors mentioned earlier). The deal was not really very complex in its structure. The company was taken over for a nominal sum, lock, stock and barrel, and the extra funding provided by the banks bought enough time to trade out of the situation.

The company is continuing to develop and is now a small group consisting of five different companies, one of which is in Sweden. We hope to become a public company on the USM within the next three years and we are constantly trying to improve profit margins to keep the company on that track.

11

Roger Malcolm/Bellwinch – The Buyout After a Turnaround

Robert (better known as Ron) King had been with Tarmac plc for 18 years when he decided to quit and set up on his own in 1981. Then chief executive of Tarmac's housebuilding subsidiary John McLean & Sons Ltd, he had no great ambition to return to a large company. Together with his wife, Audrey, he bought some land near Swindon and started building under the name Ron King Homes. His total capital at that time was £140,000.

That same summer, he was approached by property development company Capital and Counties, which owned an ailing housebuilders, Roger Malcolm Ltd. Would King join them as part-time managing director to turn the builder around, to the point where it could be floated to realize their investment. King said no at first, then relented as the C&C board persisted. 'My mind wasn't fully occupied running my own business', he says. 'I told them I'd do the job for two years to bring the company back to profit.'

Roger Malcolm was founded in 1932 by a highly respected builder, R.M. Raymond. It operated successfully in North West London until it was sold to Greenham Securities when Raymond wanted to retire. Greenham was subsequently acquired for its property portfolio by Capital and Counties. C&C did not want to be in the building business; Roger Malcolm simply came with the deal as part of the baggage.

During the 1970s, property companies had more than enough worries of their own to consider. Roger Malcolm was largely ignored. Only when C&C's top management started looking closely at the housebuilding operation in the early 1980s did they realize how seriously it had got out of hand. Among the skeletons that fell out of the cupboard was the realization that C&C had been lending to Roger Malcolm without charging interest. Using these cheap loans, the company had bought land all over the place. 'The managers didn't understand that this business is about selling', says King. 'They had a large number of houses being built that hadn't even got reservations on them. There were quality problems, too. C&C recognized that their public image would suffer if they didn't get the company working properly.'

King was given a free hand to do what was necessary. Most of the previous board were asked to leave and so was half the workforce. King recalls:

> The company had a lot of poorly built, poorly designed units in less than ideal locations. In two weeks I went around seeing every site and reviewing it. Then I dismissed 37 of the 75 staff. I kept the sales and production directors for the while and asked the development director, who was due to retire, to stay on for continuity's sake.

Searching for a new production director, King soon found a former Tarmac colleague, George Webb, who had preceded him in going it alone. George Webb Homes Ltd was operating successfully in and around Southampton. Webb joined Roger Malcolm in 1982. As King put it:

> We had to spend a lot of money to put the company right. The first year we lost money. We had a £1.6 million deficit on the balance sheet, supported by a loan from C&C. The company had large amounts of land in Yeovil and Maidstone. Eventually we sold the Yeovil site to a local builder at a profit. The Maidstone site we sold part of and applied for a change of use for the rest, from domestic to retail. When change of use was granted, we were able to sell at a £3 million profit.

One of the major tasks facing King was changing attitudes among the staff. The salesman at the company's Milton Keynes showhouse was very proud of having saved money by doing a deal with MFI. The do-it-yourself furniture company had provided the units free as a promotional exercise. King spent £50,000 bringing in American designers to produce kitchens and bathrooms of exceptional quality and appearance. Sales shot up.

> We had to convince them that our business is about selling and that the customer is paramount. It took time to instil that philosophy. Now our site staff help move the customer into the house and even order the milk.

All this time, King's and Webb's own companies were prospering. By the end of King's two-year contract, Ron King Homes was building 50 homes a year. Roger Malcolm was 'a leaner, profitable company with talented people' and was starting to acquire land once more. King's talents as a buyer of land and a seller of houses were well complemented by Webb's ability to make sure the houses were built to a high standard and within budget. C&C negotiated a deal for them to stay on, and offered King an option on 10 per cent of the shares, which he accepted.

C&C still intended to take Roger Malcolm to market, but had not set a date. In January 1985, King suggested it would be easier to sell directly to him. The C&C board were not happy at the idea, believing they could get a higher price with a flotation. However, King's shareholding gave him a leverage. Neither he nor C&C could sell out without the other's approval.

King turned for advice to a newly formed venture capital firm, Causeway Capital. They took up the case with C&C and eventually agreed a price. The negotiations took almost six months. Causeway put together a consortium of eleven other institutional investors and acted as arbiter between them and the two managers. 'The difficult part of the negotiation was not wanting to give away too much of the equity', says King. 'They were not convinced we could produce the profits I was predicting. So we agreed a ratchet arrangement, which would increase our shareholding to what we considered reasonable.' The ratchet allowed for a gradual increase of King's and Webb's shareholding from 25 to 39 per cent if profit targets were met.

To effect the buyout, King bought an off-the-shelf company, Bellwinch Ltd. Bellwinch acquired Ron King Homes and George Webb Ltd. A capital injection then provided working capital and £6.7 million to acquire the remaining shares of Roger Malcolm.

King's business plan called for flotation of Bellwinch in three years.

In the event, the required level of profitability was reached in 18 months, by which time the company was producing more than 500 housing units a year. The flotation was by a placing rather than an offer for sale (even at £400,000, a placing was about half the cost) and allowed those institutions that wanted to cash in their stake to do so. In all, some £11.75 million was raised by the placing, of which £2.75 million went towards repaying the redeemable preference element of the share structure. By coincidence, the flotation, which valued the company at £36.75 million, was exactly six years to the day after King accepted the reins of Roger Malcolm.

Bellwinch continues to grow, helped by a relatively buoyant housing market. It has concentrated its activities on the M3 and M4/M25 corridors and in London's docklands, where it was one of the first companies to take the plunge – a bold but highly profitable move. 'I regard myself as extraordinarily lucky', says King. 'George and I have both had tremendous support from our families. And the two of us have a very close understanding about the business. Two of the keys to our success have been total trust in each other and a determination to win.'

12

FMA – Buyout With a Continuing Distribution Tie

The experience of the FMA Group illustrates the important role of advisers/investors in a management buyout. FMA specializes in liquid flow measurement and control. The directors who achieved the buyout had been working as managers with the parent company, Geosource Ltd for some years, in engineering and marketing, but had little direct experience of financial management.

The FMA Group was formed in 1981 when the three founder directors purchased the Flow Measurement and Control Division of Geosource UK Ltd. Initially, Geosource offered the division for sale to a German company, on the advice of the UK group's vice-president.

John Napper, then the general sales manager (Europe), identifies two main reasons leading to Geosource's decision to sell. He explains that Geosource had treated the small flow measurement and control division in the same way as its major profit centres, expecting a level of administration and financial reporting it found very difficult to comply with. The managers, he says, became too busy working out percentage deviation from targets to manage effectively.

Secondly, the operation was never successful in Geosource's view because of the size of central charges for administrative and financial services. Napper, now chairman of FMA, claims that, without the heavy overheads, a more accurate view would have been gained of the division's profitability. At the time of the bid, the division was breaking even on a turnover of nearly £1 million.

Geosource was surprised by the management bid placed by Napper, the only director named, which rivalled the bid from the German company. Napper's offer was rejected as too low. Shortly afterwards, however, negotiations also broke down with the German bidder.

The management group's second bid was made six months later. Napper had toured around the High Street banks. They demanded security for twice the sum to be loaned. Then Napper approached 3i, and a provisional financial agreement was rapidly achieved. Napper met 3i on a Friday afternoon and had reached agreement by the following Tuesday. The directors raised considerable finance themselves, but they did not have to provide additional personal guarantees to 3i, which lent to the company rather than to the individual managers.

For the next offer, 3i representatives were in on the negotiations. Napper found this to be a useful bargaining support, as 3i was physical proof of an outside agency keeping a watch on the price. There were tough negotiations for four or five months. The management group gradually increased its offer until an agreement was reached.

An important part of the deal was that the buyout would acquire the UK distributorship of the largest element of the Geosource Group, Smith Meter. For Geosource this brought the UK company into line with the rest of its global operations, all of which (apart from South Africa and the UK) used distributors rather than an internal marketing arm. For FMA it provided an immediate base of business in a market the managers knew.

Napper cites the importance of 3i in providing financial advice. In particular, it advised that while the original sum asked for would cover the purchase price, it would not sufficiently cover running costs, or provide scope for further acquisitions. The amount of the loan was therefore increased.

Napper points out that the speed of growth of the group was helped by taking on an already growing company and, significantly, by starting with a clean slate, without inheriting the debtors of the previous company. It also benefited from an amicable relationship with Geosource with whom it now trades on a normal commercial basis.

The first acquisition began almost immediately after the buyout was achieved, starting with a bulk meter calibration and service organization from Dresser Europe UK in July 1982. FMA has since broadened its base into hygienic metering and increased its mechanical expertise by buying Maurer Instruments, manufacturers of turbine flowmeters and meter calibration, in November 1986.

The group has also undertaken a number of in-house innovations including the forming of a specialist computer company in July 1983, to respond to the increased importance of microprocessors in metering, and a team of software writers. It also runs a consultancy service to deal with customers' flow measurement problems and has established FMA (Process Equipment) to provide specialist advice in the area of valves and filtration. On an expected turnover of £6 million this year, FMA's profit before tax is estimated at 7.5–8 per cent.

13

Financial Weekly – The Buyout as an Escape From the Parental Grasp

Financial Weekly is one of those good ideas that has taken a long time to turn good. Launched by Trafalgar House in 1979, as a result of Victor Matthews' failure to acquire *Investors Chronicle* from the Pearson Group, it worked its way through several editors in the following two years. Among them were William Davis, former City editor of both *The Guardian* and the *Evening Standard*, and Stephen Hugh-Jones from *The Economist*.

By the time Trafalgar decided to 'demerge' its publishing interests into Fleet Holdings in the Autumn of 1981, *Financial Weekly* was in trouble. It had never turned a profit and the chances of it doing so under its then management seemed increasingly slim. When the publication was launched in February 1979, it operated from plush premises in Holborn and had a staff of 54. As the revenues failed to come in the magazine was merged with another loss-maker, *Accountants Weekly*, and a free circulation to 62,000 accountants added to its subscription base. The plan was to attract a high level of classified advertising. In practice, the tabloid newspaper never reached its targets.

Seeing the writing on the wall, several of the journalists, led by Tom Lloyd, the news editor, began to plan a management buyout. By the time Fleet Holdings announced the magazine's closure in April 1982, they already had a business plan but were still seeking finance.

If the magazine were off the streets for more than a short period, the chances of survival would be much reduced. So speed was of the essence. Enter press baron Robert Maxwell, whose British Printing and Communication Corporation was hungry for periodical titles. The staff were left with 25 per cent of the equity. Hugh-Jones, who was on holiday while all this was happening, returned home to find himself out of a job. The publication was relaunched under a new editor, Ray Heath, with the loss of only one issue. Tom Lloyd became deputy editor and subsequently editor when Heath left.

For *Financial Weekly* the BPCC solution was a case of out of the frying pan into the fire. Here is how the publication described the 'honeymoon' period:

> *Financial Weekly* continued to struggle under Maxwell, largely because of a chronic lack of managerial ability and publishing experience within BPCC. *Financial Weekly* had six managing directors and five advertising managers in the first eighteen months of Maxwell's proprietorship. For various reasons the staff never subscribed for their shares.

By now, Maxwell had acquired the Mirror Group and had more than enough publications to play with. Lloyd says, 'I had asked Maxwell for leave to seek finance for a buyout on a number of occasions. The first time he said, "I never sell anything and I never close anything". Later, after he had closed *The Health Services* (formerly *The Times Health Supplement*), he said, "I never sell anything".'

Then, suddenly, at the end of July 1984, Lloyd received a memorandum from Maxwell stating that a cash bid had been received for *Financial Weekly*. The staff had ten days to match the bid if they wanted to buy the title.

The identity of this mystery bidder was never revealed. Lloyd, his deputy editor, Cathy Gunn, and City editor, Mihir Bose, secretly approached Clive Thornton, chief executive of Abbey National Building Society, and invited him to join the buyout consortium. Thornton had just been publicly ejected from his job as chairman of Mirror Group Newspapers and was not unduly well-disposed towards Maxwell. These negotiations had to be carried on in secret. The *Financial Weekly* team assigned all the characters in the plot codenames from *The Lord of the Rings*. Thornton, the white knight, became Gandalf; the company Hobbit Ltd; Maxwell became Sauron, with Maxwell House, inevitably, the dark land of Mordor.

The major problem for the buyout team was not knowing what price they were bidding against, nor, indeed, whether they were in an auction, or whether the prize would go to the highest bidder. Was Maxwell using them to drive up the price to someone else? Or was there, as they increasingly began to suspect, no mystery bidder at all? Three bids were made and all were rejected. Then Maxwell suddenly announced that he was going to keep the publication after all. It seemed that all the buyout team's efforts were wasted. Morale within the publication plummeted. Then, just before the end of the year, Lloyd met two representatives of a Swedish financial publishing company, Affarsvarlden. As the publication itself describes the meeting:

> The personal chemistry, aided by Courage Directors bitter, was excellent. Affarsvarlden was looking for a UK title to buy; the discussion was about what might have been.

Early in the New Year Maxwell appointed his 26–year-old son Kevin as *Financial Weekly*'s seventh managing director. Kevin persuaded his father to re-open the buyout option. Lloyd immediately made contact with Affarsvarlden, reawakened Clive Thornton's interest, retained the services of a merchant bank, and began negotiating.

The staff themselves had very little capital, so outside investment was essential. Loanstock was not a viable option, as the publication had never made any money and gearing up would simply have made the cashflow position even more difficult. The Swedes agreed to put up the additional cash needed to finance the buyout and to relaunch the paper as a magazine. Further tranches of capital would be available if needed as the magazine worked its way to profitability. The staff could exercise a stock option at a later date, if they so wished.

The Swedes were concerned not to take away the incentive of ownership from the staff, so they were happy to settle for 45 per cent ownership. Thornton retained 25 per cent, Lloyd took 10 per cent, having invested an inheritance of his own, and other key staff took 6 per cent. The remaining 14 per cent went into trust, to form the basis of the employee stock option scheme.

But why go to Sweden for cash? Part of the answer lies in the genuine synergy between the two companies. Affarsvarlden had achieved a strong market position in Scandinavia with a similar publication, starting with nothing and achieving a £1 million profit in 1984; it had a mixture of hands-off and hands-on management that appealed strongly to the *Financial Weekly* staff; and it was not greedy. The *Financial Weekly* team particularly liked the way in which Affarsvarlden wanted gradually to reduce its equity holding to put more capital into the hands of the staff. 'They know all about "know-how" companies', says Lloyd. 'They know that you need to lock senior staff in, to keep costs down. Our culture is very similar to theirs.'

The second reason for seeking cash from Sweden was that it simply was not available in Britain. As Lloyd says:

> We tried to get venture capital in the UK. Although I knew some of the venture capital guys quite well, I was very disappointed. I don't think they realized what wonderful operational gearing there is in publishing once you pass break-even. Most of them moaned about our being a one product company.

Negotiations were finally completed on press day, 31 April 1985. 'We held the front page', recalls Lloyd. 'The deputy editor was at the typesetter, waiting to see if we could announce the deal in that issue.'

The publication kept to the same formula until later that year. Some months before the buyout, Maxwell had trumpeted to the trade that *Financial Weekly* would change its format from tabloid to normal magazine size. He first gave a date of October 1984, then February 1985, then April 1985. It did not happen. Aware that there was now a credibility problem, *Financial Weekly* had to keep the next promise it made. It promised a September changeover and delivered.

Affarsvarlden gave a Swedish director, Ronald Fagerfjall, special responsibility for turning the company around and spending a significant amount of his time in the *Financial Weekly* offices. Thornton put in considerable effort on the advertising management side. Now that the venture has a full-time managing editor and a full-time advertising manager, their direct input is less intense.

Financial Weekly, at the time of writing, is still not profitable. However, it claims to be well on target to reach profitability. The staff, and particularly Lloyd the editor, see the experience as an adventure. He admits:

> There's an opportunity cost. I'm getting paid only half what I'm worth on the open market. But if I compare what I've gained with what I've sacrificed, I've given up very little. The big thing about a management buyout is that it's fun. You haven't got guys like Maxwell breathing down your neck. And there's a tremendous satisfaction in knowing that we have achieved what Trafalgar House and Maxwell failed to do.

For some, the hook has not been sufficiently well baited. Deputy editor Cathy Gunn has left for a job with more jam today; so have the city editor, production editor and features editor. In practice, however, this staff turnover is no greater – and probably somewhat lower – than in financial journalism in general. 'At one stage we were seen as a training ground, where people would gain valuable experience before moving on', says Lloyd. 'Now we are trying to make it increasingly attractive to stay.'

14

Hornby – A Buyout That Failed

The name Hornby has a special meaning for generations of men and boys. The famous 00 train sets have a fanatical following. Adam Faith, the King of Saudi Arabia, Arthur Hailey and Andrew Lloyd Webber are all model train mad. Yet Frank Hornby, the originator of the company, started out with another, equally famous and well-loved toy – Meccano.

Hornby, a Liverpool meat importer, wanted to create a toy that was both educational and fun. Several months of experimentation in his workshop at home produced the ingenious metal strips, which could be bolted together to form almost any kind of machine or construction a child (or his father) could conceive. Hornby patented the idea, took a partner and started production in that same workshop. The toy took off so rapidly that it swept the market, needing larger and larger production premises.

By the end of the First World War, however, Hornby recognized that a one-product company was vulnerable. Casting round for other products to make, he fastened on model railways, then a market dominated by the Germans. The first Hornby trains were basically Meccano kits with additions and did not resemble any particular train. Larger than the current 00 size, they ran by clockwork and were made primarily of tinplate.

The first Hornby train was followed by models of real engines, including 'The Flying Scotsman'. While these too sold in large numbers, Hornby was stung by the criticism of purists that the trains had all kinds of design inaccuracies. From then on, the company aimed to achieve a scaled-down representation as close to the real thing as it was possible to make. Now collectors' items with price tags running into hundreds of pounds and sometimes considerably more, these original Hornby trains gradually gave way to electric-powered models. The smaller 00 gauge, introduced in 1938, two years after Hornby's death, made it easier to plan realistic layouts and the demand grew rapidly for accessories such as tunnels, bridges, stations, signal boxes – and scaled-down cars.

It was these scaled-down cars that led directly to another famous line of toys – Dinky. Dinky cars dominated their section of the market until the 1950s when competitors such as Matchbox began to erode their position. At the same time, cheaper plastic trains, produced by a company called Rovex Plastics, began to make inroads into the model train business. The plastic trains were half the price of Meccano's tinplate ones, but the Meccano management refused to acknowledge the threat, insisting that quality would out.

By 1964, Meccano was close to collapse. It was sold to Lines Brothers, then the largest toymaker in Britain. Lines also owned Rovex. It merged the two companies, scrapped tinplate model production and called the new model railway company Triang Hornby. Meccano construction kits and Dinky toys were separated from the model railway operations. Then a new craze swept the market. Scalextric, with its fast moving racing cars, made model railways seem sedate and unexciting. Lines Brothers, already under siege in other sectors of its market, went under in 1971, selling out to Dunbee Combex-Marx, which produced Scalextric. It combined the Scalextric and Hornby operations under one roof at Margate.

In 1981, Dunbee Combex-Marx continued the pattern by going into receivership itself. At the time, Rovex/Hornby was the jewel in the Dunbee crown, the only really profitable part of the group. Karl Mueller, the managing director, tramped the City trying to arrange backing for a buyout. After a year, he was able, with the help of Guidehouse, to put together a deal with a consortium of investors led by Citicorp Venture Capital. The enthusiasm of the City for investing in such a troubled industry was not high. Mueller and his colleagues bought an off-the-shelf company, Wiltminster Ltd, used it as a holding company, and then formed Hornby Hobbies Ltd, which bought the assets and trade of Rovex from the receiver. The £5.5 million buyout was one of the largest at that time. The deal involved a mixture of equity and loans secured against the assets, with the purchase price being below asset value.

It all looked straightforward from then on. The company had two major market leading products – Hornby model trains and Scalextric; its main problem was how to produce sufficient product to meet demand. The managers felt no need to diversify.

The management team's forecast to justify the investors' confidence was that the company would make a profit of £2 million pre-tax in its first year. In the event, sales turnover was halved by an onslaught from an unexpected source. Video games and home computers burst on to the market, causing Hornby Hobbies to turn in a loss of £1.7 million.

For the investing institutions, this was a disaster. One option was to sell off the company for whatever they could get for it and take a loss on their investment. The alternative was to diversify. They assembled a £10 million rescue package and removed Mueller. 'They felt the management needed to be changed to take them into different sectors of the toy market', says the current finance director, Alan Cox. Soon after Mueller's departure, the then finance director was offered a senior position elsewhere and he, too, departed. Jack Strowger, former managing director of electronics company Thorn-EMI, who had joined the board as a non-executive, part-time chairman, stayed on and became a full-time executive chairman. (He had thought Hornby would be an interesting hobby for his retirement, a one day a month task.) A new managing director, Keith Ness, was appointed. He brought in a complete new team of sales director, marketing director and manufacturing director, all of whom had expertise in girls' toys.

The new management team was faced with a barrage of problems. The first was the sheer scale of the interest charges the company was paying. The original buyout consisted of a relatively modest amount of equity capital, £600,000 and £3.6 million of debt in the form of loan notes. The remaining £1.3 million came from ordinary bank shares. The loan repayments amounted to a crippling £500,000 and more per annum. This high level of gearing meant that cash was perilously short and it was inevitable that the company made losses between 1982 and 1984.

Equally daunting was the strength of the competition from US-owned companies, which were spending heavily on product development and television promotion. 'We were in a desperate condition', says Cox. Against this background, it was surprising that the company was able to attract such a high calibre of new management. Only a small amount of equity became available to them when the previous management was fully disentangled from the company. The salaries offered were good, but not exceptional. Their primary motive for taking such risky jobs appears to have been the sheer challenge of turning round a household-name company.

To stem the losses, Strowger and Ness took an axe to the overheads, halving them in 18 months from £9 million to £4.5 million. The work-force of 1200 was cut to 350. As Cox says:

> All the indirect departments were cut in half at the minimum. Everyone said it couldn't be done, but we did it. We sold everything that was not bolted down or needed immediately. Morale was low but there was a remarkable fighting spirit. At one stage employees' families were coming in over the weekend to work on the packing line so we could get the product out of the door. We developed new products during the day and cut back the company at night. We were working 24 hours a day.

The first new product, Flower Fingers, did not achieve much market penetration because the company could not afford to promote them and the market was not prepared for such products from a hobby company. Hornby tried again, this time capitalizing on its past with a range of clockwork trains for the very young and making merchandising deals on popular television characters such as Postman Pat. The real breakthrough came from a product designed on the floor of an office in Hong Kong. Called Flower Fairies, it was an instant success, especially after it won the National Association of Toymakers' award for the best toy of 1984.

The turnaround was helped, too, by the fickleness of the toy market. The boom in home computers and video games faded as quickly as it had come. Sales of model trains picked up with a new showing of the film *The Railway Children* on television, and Scalextric benefited from renewed interest in speedway racing. By 1986, the company was in a fit state to be floated on the Unlisted Securities Market. It had already paid back the first of six equal tranches of debt and the flotation of 4.5 million £1 shares allowed it to dispose of the remaining debt, together with its interest burden.

Hornby has now restored its employment level to 850, more than double the number at the time of greatest crisis. ‘We went round to the homes of former employees and asked if they would like to come back’, says Cox. ‘Many of them did.’

15

Exacta Circuits – The Model Buyout of a Non-core Business

Making printed circuit boards is a highly specialized business, with only a few European players able to achieve state-of-the-art production in bulk. Exacta Circuits is proving to be one of the most commercially stable big producers, particularly since its transfer of ownership from STC to the management team.

Exacta was established in Galashiels in the 1960s by two entrepreneurs, Robert Currie and Ken Mill. They sold out in 1974 to STC, which was then a subsidiary of the US-based international conglomerate ITT. STC's interest was in securing supplies for its switching exchange equipment and it took up 50–60 per cent of Exacta's production capacity for several years. Then, in the early 1980s, the demand for STC's exchange equipment fell until, by 1985, only 12 per cent of Exacta's production went to STC, with Exacta expanding its customer base from telecommunications into computers. At the same time, STC as a whole was in difficulties. Its chairman, Sir Kenneth Corfield, had been removed as profits dipped and the City lost confidence in the company's ability to perform in the long-term, intensively competitive international markets.

As its share price dipped below 70, Arthur Walsh the new STC chief executive appointed a former senior manager from Dunlop, Ken Gardener, to identify those businesses that were not central to the group's activities and to sell them off for the best price. A list of more than thirty companies was drawn up.

Exacta was one of the companies that made its way on to Gardener's list. It was – on paper at least – unprofitable; it was in a difficult market where STC no longer had a significant interest in controlling supplies; and, in STC terms, it was a relatively small business, turning over just less than £20 million (1985) a year. Derrick Bumpsteed, who had been sent from the South East to turn Exacta round, accepted the job knowing that there were rumours of a sell-off. 'I arrived in August 1985', he recalls, 'when STC was saying that a sell-off was no more than a vague possibility. Two months later they said it was realistic. We immediately started to talk to the auditors.'

It was Gardener who raised the possibility of a buyout formally. Bumpsteed and his six most senior colleagues all met at a hotel that weekend, to discuss whether this was an offer they could not refuse. They decided it was and told STC they would like to pursue an offer.

'We had already been preparing a five year business plan for STC', says Bumpsteed. 'Now we recast the plan and put some meat on it.' The revised version presented a very different picture, not because the managers had got their figures wrong before, but because a change in ownership had a radical effect on profitability. 'It's part of the problem of being a big company,' explains Bumpsteed. 'Exacta was always making losses because it was carrying very big overheads. We weren't a big company saleswise, but we were always being hit for hefty central charges. When we dug into the figures, however, the business was always generating a lot of cash.'

The idea of a buyout had been raised among his colleagues by the outgoing managing director, but he was not able to inspire them to follow him. But the seed had been planted and by the time Bumpsteed, a much stronger character, had begun to settle in, the management team was much more positive about the possibility. Ian Lang, the technical director, recalls:

> We were attracted to the idea for two reasons. Firstly, because we knew it had been done elsewhere – ten years ago it was so uncommon it wouldn't have entered our minds – and secondly because we were increasingly dissatisfied with the way we were being treated by STC. STC judged us to be a non-core business and expected high profits in addition to their central charges. That was very difficult to do in a strongly competitive business where price is important. They failed to realize that they were putting the wrong pressures on us, insisting on high profits when the marketplace couldn't give the necessary volume of sales. By

the time the STC management changed and they began to treat us differently, we had already begun to feel we might as well run the company for ourselves. A year later, I think STC would have kept us, because its attitude to non-core businesses is very different now. We were very lucky in our timing.

There were three major hurdles Bumpsteed and his colleagues had to overcome. The first was raising the cash; the second creating a management team that could deliver the goods to the investors; and the third was to convince STC to sell to the managers rather than an outside bidder.

STC's auditors and advisers were Arthur Andersen in London. The Exacta managers went with STC's blessing to Arthur Andersen in Edinburgh and were reassured that there would be no conflict of interests. Andersen's passed them on to 3i, who agreed to become the lead investor in a deal that was estimated to require around £10 million in equity and loanstock.

As this would be Scotland's largest management buyout, says Charles Peal, the 3i City office Investment Director who handled the project, 'we thought it would be good to make it an exclusive Scottish deal, given that Glasgow, Edinburgh, Perth and Dundee all have huge financial resources. To begin with, we were very successful. The Bank of Scotland came in very swiftly. They were very quick to understand what we were doing. We had a champion there who knew the company and its managers well.'

When it came to raising investment cash from other Scottish institutions, however, Peal met with mixed interest. There were several reasons for this. First, the electronics sector as a whole was in the doldrums and out of favour at that time. Secondly, the Scottish institutions made clear their preference for investing in quoted companies. Thirdly, many of them were already investors in a major printed circuit manufacturer and felt there would be a conflict of interest. Also, Prestwick's recently floated shares had rapidly dropped from 100p to less than 40p. Would Exacta's fortunes follow the same pattern?

3i, to its credit, refused to be panicked. 'Our confidence in this team was not shaken', says Peal. 'We went round and talked to key customers. We asked DEC, IBM, Wang and other such companies about their plans and ambitions. They told us that Exacta was not a company to be worried about; even though investors were busy selling electronics shares, the prospects for Exacta and its key customers were still good.' Comparing Exacta with its competitors, 3i was impressed by the strength of its customer list. Whether by luck or good judgement, the company had tied its fortunes to the strong European subsidiaries of major US computer businesses.

Extending the syndication strategy to London brought a much more positive response. Even so, by the date the deal was due to be signed, there remained one investment tranche of £528,000 to be placed. 3i showed its confidence in the project once again by taking that tranche itself, increasing its stake by 50 per cent. It was able to sell this final tranch on to the Prudential a few weeks later.

It was all a bit bewildering to Exacta's managers. Says technical director, Ian Long, 'I felt like a small pawn in a big game. There were a lot of other people involved and we had to be guided by our advisers. They did a great deal we couldn't have done, such as making introductions, and showing us how to present our case.'

The second problem, the composition of the team, was perhaps the most difficult of all. There was no doubt in Bumpsteed's mind that he had to present a strong dynamic team that could inspire confidence in both the investors and the workforce. 'When you sell to investors, you sell the team', he declares. Decisions had to be made about who qualified to become members of the executive team. In sorting out the company for STC, Bumpsteed would almost certainly have wanted to make some senior-level personnel changes. Now the necessity was even more urgent. Three of the people who met at the hotel were told bluntly that they were not going to become directors. One quit when the buyout was concluded; a second quit a couple of months later; a third accepted the situation and has since become a strong supporter within the management team, even though he has no equity stake. 'It wasn't as acrimonious as it might have been', says Bumpsteed. 'People tend to bow to the inevitable.'

'It's very instructive to watch a team emerge', says Peal. The ability of the chief executive to take these tough decisions is one of the characteristics an investor should look out for, because it provides useful insights into how well the team will cope with difficult issues in the future. The decisions made by Bumpsteed and his colleagues were closely in line with those that 3i would have advised them to make. Peal explains:

> If you see a team about to make a correct decision, you don't push too hard. It is the boss who has to make the decision. It gave us confidence in him, because it was a tough decision to make, not least because he liked the people who left.

The resulting top team was attractive from an investment point of view because it was well balanced between marketing and technology. There was even a balance between Scots and English, with two of each on the board. A potential weakness in the financial control area was removed by hiring a first-class Scots financial director with international experience.

The third problem – competitive bidders – was complicated by the fact that Gardener had circulated a long form report on Exacta, prepared by Arthur Andersen, to a number of serious enquirers. These included Olivetti, which wanted greater penetration of the UK market, and Prestwick, Exacta's closest competitor, which is also located in Scotland.

STC had made it clear that it preferred to sell to the existing management, but that it had a responsibility to its shareholders to obtain a good price. So Gardener kept tweaking the negotiating team's nose about the presence of alternative bidders. 3i carried out detailed investigations into how real these bids were and thought it relatively unlikely that Prestwick would be able to raise the cash, given its own problems. Nonetheless, the threat from Olivetti obliged them to raise the offer from one pegged at net assets to one that represented a small premium on net assets.

Having reached agreement with STC that the offer was fair, 3i played its own trump card. Given that the other bids could not proceed without revealing commercially sensitive information and exposing Exacta's strategy and technology to its competitors, STC must either say no to the buyout or call the other bidders off. Gardener agreed to the buyout. Both sides were now committed to wrapping up a deal as quickly as possible.

By this time, recalls Bumpsteed, 'the workforce was getting twitchy. We had had a redundancy programme in November and a pay freeze in January. We split the workforce into groups of 20 and told them what was happening, that whatever happened the company was not going under. We also made a point of going out to customers and giving them the same message. Of course, they were hearing from the competition that we were in trouble, so we had to make it clear that nothing basic was changing.' The financial advisers of one of the other bidders then began to make noises to 3i about the possibility that their client might take a share of the action – an option the Exacta team and its advisers were not prepared to countenance.

The deal stitched together by 3i gave the four key managers a 15 per cent shareholding, rising to 25 per cent if they achieved profit targets or took the company to the market. STC declared itself happy with the outline sale arrangements and both sides turned the details over to their respective lawyers. 'It was the legal stuff that held everything up,' says Bumpsteed. 'It kept going backwards and forwards. STC was insistent on what it wanted included, so was 3i.'

Unlike so many buyouts, however, it was clear that the deal was indeed going to happen. Bumpsteed found himself gradually spending more and more time on the buyout, from 30 per cent when it was first mooted to 100 per cent in the final six weeks. The other members of the management team only became heavily involved in this latter period. As Bumpsteed says:

> The experience has made all of us grow. We have a broader concept of the business as a whole and a lot of the barriers between departments have come down. One of the big differences is that the decision base is here and not in London. In a big company there is always someone above to pass the decision up to, to make them worry as well. Now the buck really does stop here.

Reaction from the workforce, suspicious at first, was positive once it was understood that the directors had put their own money in. Says Lang:

> People in the town and the factory see us differently now. Two years ago they saw us as the people in the middle, with no power to change things. Now they see us as the accountable ones and seem happy to put their faith in us to maintain their jobs.

Lang has noticed changes in himself.

> My decision-making is sharper, because I have more financial responsibility. Although I always took financial aspects into account before, as a technical guy I gave less importance to the need to be profitable than I do now.

One aspect of the buyout that surprised Lang was the cost, some

£300,000 including duties and professional fees. But, he admits, 'I don't see how we could have done it without our advisers'.

In the first year after the buyout, Exacta invested £1.4 million in new equipment. 'That would have been difficult in STC, strapped as it was for cash', says Bumpsteed. 'It was very unlikely we'd have got all the investment in plant that we needed. We were just swamped in the larger company.'

Along with the rest of the industry, Exacta suffered from a downturn in orders in 1986. Because it was producing specialist circuit boards for blue chip customers, however, it weathered the storm better than its competitors, generating cash and making substantial profits while others went into the red. All through this period, Bumpsteed and his colleagues made a point of keeping the investors closely informed – something he feels is essential whatever the state of business. 'It would be easy to say, "They've only put in money; we've got to run the business." But you may need them later, so it pays to keep them in touch.'

Part of the agreement concerned the appointment of non-executive directors. 3i would appoint a chairman, subject to acceptance by the management. The other investors could also appoint a director to the board. 'We wanted someone who would give advice and ideas', says Bumpsteed. 'We weren't looking for someone with a knowledge of printed circuit board manufacture – after all, we know more about that than anyone else would be likely to. So we opted for someone from a completely different sector of industry.' They chose James Hann, an entrepreneur with his own business serving offshore oil companies.

For the second non-executive director, four candidates were introduced by the investor group. 'There was a danger that one of the investors would appoint someone who would be "his man", simply reporting back to them. That would inevitably have led to split meetings. We needed someone who would really contribute and be his own man,' says Bumpsteed. Peter Lawson, a former consultant with PA Technology, fitted the bill.

Exacta's business now looks distinctly healthy, with money in the bank and good prospects of a flotation in due course. Bumpsteed recognizes, however, that being a one-product company has its dangers and that the company would be less vulnerable to cyclical factors in the computer industry if it had a second string to its bow. Its medium-term plans therefore include diversification into another, related high-tech activity.

In many ways, the Exacta experience typifies the most straightforward kind of leveraged buyout. It involves a tough and intelligent, well-balanced management team, a well-disposed vendor and a highly supportive financial adviser. The fact that even this combination had to overcome a series of difficulties illustrates just how complex a less ideal buyout can be.

16

National Freight – An Employee Buyout on the Grand Scale

The following account, one of the most detailed reports of a major buyout by the chief executive responsible, originally appeared in the journal *Long Range Planning* and is reproduced here by permission of Pergamon Press.

When the employees of National Freight were offered the opportunity to acquire the ownership of their business, in February 1982, by buying shares, we had a vision for the future of the company. As I wrote in the Prospectus at that time, we believed, as we do today, that

> by creating a company controlled and owned mainly by employees, we were launching a new kind of industrial enterprise. We believed that this would help to get rid of the conflicts between management and workers traditional to British Industry – the 'us and them' attitude. In its place would be a new attitude of cooperation which should lead to improved efficiency, better prospects for employment and better profitability.

In working hard to put flesh on that vision, we also knew that commercial success was essential - not only to retain the confidence of our investors, most of whom worked in the business, but also to invest in the long-term future of the enterprise and, of course, to reward shareholders for their investment.

Our results for 1983–84, our third year of operation, demonstrate how successful we have been in building a strong, profitable and expanding business (Table 1). This success has been fuelled by record levels of investment in NFC, but the hidden 'plus factor' has

Table 1. How NFC turnover and trading profit have moved in the 3 years since the buyout

Three-Year Comparisons of NFC Turnover and Trading Profit*

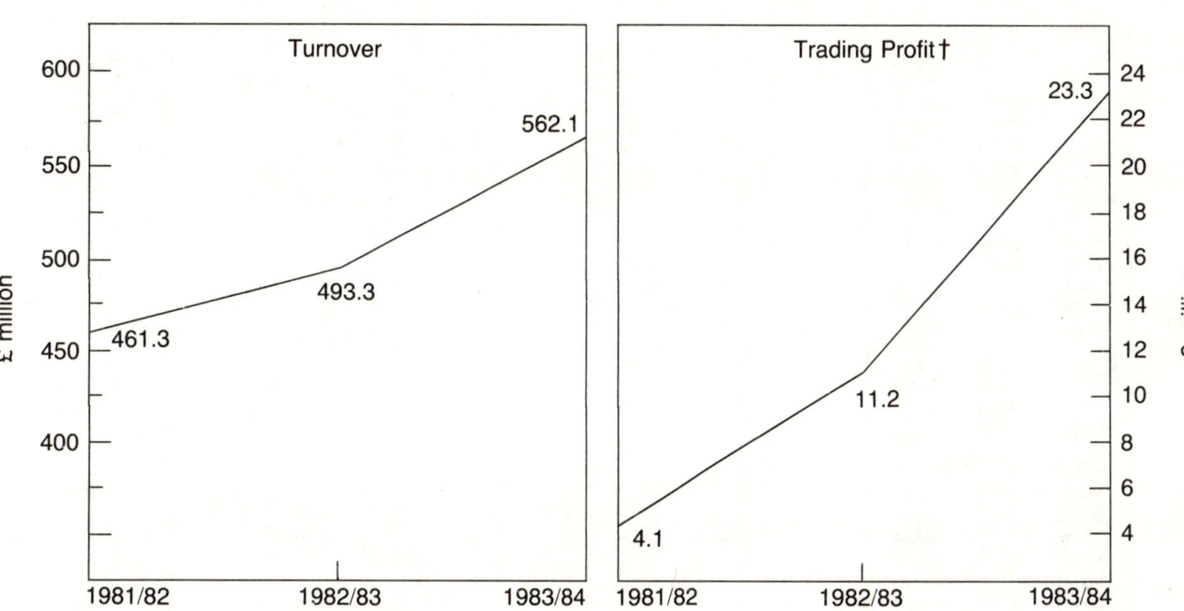

*1981/82 and 82/83 for 52 weeks, 1983/84 for 53 weeks.

† Trading profit after deducting redundancy payments. In 1983/84 costs of £1.3m relating to properties held for disposal were charged against profits on disposal of land and buildings. In earlier years such costs were charged in arriving at trading profits.

undoubtedly been employee ownership and, here again, we have worked hard to bring as many employees as possible into a share in the ownership – our most recent campaign, in March this year, resulting in a further 3,000 members of our staff buying shares.

Employee ownership and professional management have proved a very powerful combination, and there is no question in my mind that a company owned by a large part of its workforce has proved immensely attractive to customers, not only as a concept but also for the expectation of better service from a highly motivated staff. While we are still seeing more buyers than sellers at each of the quarterly share-dealing days in our internal trading system, we are now having to look at the possibility of flotation on the Stock Exchange some time after February 1987 – and, most particularly, at whether we can offer an attractive investment opportunity without losing the important advantages which we believe are inherent in our particular form of ownership and control. There is no guarantee that we shall float, but I believe we have to offer the present shareholders a choice on which to vote at a future AGM.

Just what have we achieved, and how did we come to buy the business in the first place? Although the answers may not provide a blueprint for others, I think they have a great deal of significance for many parts of British industry – not least in the staff commitment which a real share in the ownership creates.

The Buyout

When we bought NC in 1982, 10,300 employees and pensioners bought shares. Today we have around 16,500 such shareholders – almost all the increase having come from more employees buying into the business. NFC employees, pensioners and their immediate families hold 83 per cent of the equity, the remaining 17 per cent being held by the syndicate of banks which lent us money for the buyout. Those who bought shares at that first opportunity in 1982 have seen their holdings increase more than 12-fold in value, so even those who bought the minimum of 100 £1 shares have seen that investment grow to £1,240. Meanwhile, dividends have increased strongly year on year.

This increase in capital value (established quarterly by chartered accountants Ernst and Whinney, in the absence of a Market quotation) has been well ahead of the FT all-share index and is shown in an accompanying table; so is the growth in dividends. As indicated earlier, the improvement in financial results, which has strongly affected the reward for investors, has come increasingly from a considerable investment programme. For example, in 1983–84 we committed over £100 million to the business – far more than ever before. Much of this was to provide the property, vehicles and equipment to meet customer demand for dedicated distribution and other contract-backed activities. We plan to exceed this level of investment in the current year and have set ourselves a target of over £500 million over the next 5 years to support the very strong growth – mainly at home but also overseas – which we are intent on achieving, not least as a basis for improved job opportunties, which we see as particularly important in an employee-owned business.

Last year for the first time we also covered all our outgoings from trading profit alone, having accepted from the time of the takeover that we would need to rely partly on property sales in the first couple of years. This situation has now changed, as the accompanying financial results table demonstrates (see Table 2): not only have total profits increased very sharply but the quality of those profits has improved, with much the biggest contribution coming from our trading activities – despite heavy losses in one section of our business.

With the growth in revenue and profit we have not only been able to begin to invest in operations abroad as well as in the UK, but have had the confidence to create a challenging long-term strategy for the business, to which I would like to return in greater detail at the end of this article. First, let me remind you about our origins.

Where we came from

As Britain's largest transport, storage, distribution and travel business, NFC was shaped by a long line of political decisions. The post-war Labour Government nationalized commercial long-distance road haulage, in 1953–56 a Conservative Government partially denationalized it, and Mrs Barbara Castle's 1968 Transport Act formed the remaining State road transport businesses into the National Freight

Table 2. A comparison of the financial results of NFC over the past 2 years (1982–83 and 1983–84) shows how a very strong increase in profitability has been accompanied by an improvement in the quality of profit—i.e. more from trading activities and much less from property disposals.

How the Consortium Performed

Profit and Loss Account for the year to 6 October 1984	**1983–1984 53 weeks £m**	1982–1983 52 weeks £m	% change
Turnover (sales of services or goods to customers)	**562·1**	493·3	+14
Less: Costs incurred (wages and salaries, hire of vehicles, fuel, licences, maintenance, depreciation, etc.)	**536·5**	477·0	+12
Trading profit	**25·6**	16·3	+57
Less: Redundancy	**(2·3)**	(5·1)	−55
Trading profit after redundancy	**23·3**	11·2	+108
Add: Profits on property disposals	**4·7**	11·6	−59
Operating profit	**28·0**	22·8	+23
Less:			
Interest on medium-term loan and overdrafts	**(11·1)**	(11·0)	
Overseas taxation	**(0·3)**	–	
Extraordinary items	**(1·3)**	(2·5)	
Minorities share of profits	**(0·5)**	(0·1)	
Dividends, paid and proposed (including cost of Advance Corporation Tax paid by the Consortium)	**(4·3)**	(2·6)	+65
Profit retained in the business	**10·5**	6·6	+59

Dividends paid on NFC shares to date

Date		Dividends paid (net) p	Amount of dividend per original £1 holding p
July 1982	Interim	4·5	4·5
Oct. 1982	Interim	4·5	4·5
March 1983	Final	3·0	3·0
March 1983	Interim	5·0	5·0
May 1983	Interim	5·0	5·0
Aug. 1983	Interim	2·5*	5·0
Nov. 1983	Interim	2·5*	5·0
March 1984	Final	2·0*	4·0
March 1984	Interim	3·0*	6·0
May 1984	Interim	1·5†	6·0
Aug. 1984	Interim	1·5†	6·0
Nov. 1984	Interim	2·8†	11·2
March 1985	Final	0·52‡	10·4
March 1985	Interim	0·56‡	11·2

*Dividend per share after script issue.
†Dividend per 50p share.
‡Dividend per 10p share.

Corporation, with the addition of the road haulage activities of British Rail, which became National Carriers.

The new Corporation operated from 1969 for 10 years, initially with large revenue grants, then with chequered financial results – some small profits in one or two of the early years, heavy losses in 1975 and, after some structural and management changes in the following year, a slow growth to reasonable profitability at trading level.

When the Conservative Party came to power in 1979 the intention was to float us on the Stock Exchange and with this in mind the Corporation, whose assets were held mainly through 40 subsidiary limited companies, was replaced by the newly created National Freight Company Limited, its equity share capital owned entirely by the government. Plans for the flotation were upset by the economic recession and its effect on our profitability, and then crucially by British Rail shutting its collected and delivered parcels service for which our National Carriers provided vehicles and drivers – an almost immediate loss of over £20 million in annual revenue.

The government was therefore advised by its merchant bankers that a successful flotation could not be considered for some 2 years – which left it in a difficult position in view of the election manifesto. We sensed that they would seek some other way to sell the business and we feared, in particular, that it might be sold piecemeal or offered to a single purchaser who could well be more interested in stripping out the substantial property assets than in continuing to run a low-margin transport business.

There were still some 25,000 employees in the business (extensive redundancy made necessary by the bad trading conditions of 1980–81 had reduced the workforce from over 30,000) and we were concerned about their future as well as the possible effects on the business of the arrival of an asset stripper. It was at this point that a group of us – senior managers – began to consider whether we might mount a bid to acquire the company. Preliminary discussions with merchant banks made it clear that unless the management was prepared to accept a position where the bid was, in practice, an institutional one with the management simply providing a small percentage on top, two things would have to happen: first, the scope would have to be widened to include the entire workforce – to obtain not only sufficient finance for success but also to obtain commitment to the change of ownership; and, secondly, institutions would need to be persuaded to lend the majority of the purchase price without acquiring a majority of the equity capital.

The resolution of these two problems was to occupy the small group of senior managers concerned for over 9 months but the principles which were established very early on, and which were subsequently published unchanged in the Prospectus, were:

- The business must be controlled by employee-investors.
- All employees, not just management, must have an equal right to invest.
- Investors should receive dividends in proportion to their investment.
- The business must be professionally managed with a board of directors responsible to the shareholders.

These were the main principles which distinguished our concept from a management buyout on the one hand and a cooperative on the other. We had quickly come to see the possibility of creating a new type of industrial enterprise.

The ownership of shares in a business does not usually imply that the shareholder has any direct involvement in the running of the business – though there have been many creditable attempts over the years to involve employees more, especially through the issue of shares as an annual bonus or as part of a company saving scheme.

I see ownership in terms of the positive ownership of a piece of the company which varies in value as the health of the company fluctuates. For me it is important, indeed crucial, to see ownership of part of the business operating as a direct factor in the control of the business.

Government, Bank and Management Reactions

In NFC we had long-established staff consultation procedures at all levels of the business, and equally well-established (and rare in the public sector), we had devolved decision-making. The management of its activities was through subsidiary operating companies, and profit centres at almost all of the hundreds of branches, and this had important implications for the success of our particular kind of privatization. We had the first practical evidence of this when we brought together our top 130 managers in 1981 to put before them, in great confidence, our proposals to buy the business from the government. A little while previously we had opened confidential discussions with Barclays Merchant Bank, who proved keen to help us, and in May, after some stringent financial and management exercises, we had put an outline of our plans to Transport Secretary Norman Fowler. He was delighted with what we suggested and gave the senior management group conditional approval to see whether we could sell the idea to the employees and make it work. At the same time he put his own legal and financial advisers to work on evaluating our proposals.

We had, of course, had to keep the NFC's Board informed of our proposals as they developed and, while the Board throughout maintained the correct stance of a body which had a legal obligation to safeguard the public interest in a State undertaking, it formally recognized our plans as perhaps the best for the future of the business and carefully 'held the ring' on behalf of the shareholder – the government.

At the highly confidential meeting of our 130 most senior managers from headquarters and operating subsidiaries throughout the NFC, the reception – after the initial startled silence – was enthusiastic. Each participant was asked to fill in, anonymously, a questionnaire which simply asked three questions:

(i) Will you be prepared to support the concept financially yourself?

(ii) How much, approximately, do you think you will be investing?

(iii) Are you prepared to endorse the concept and encourage your own people to take part?

Over 95 per cent said 'yes' to questions (i) and (iii) and the answers to question (ii) indicated that we should be able to raise the minimum equity which we had provisionally set at £5m. The amount from this group alone was likely to be well over £1m.

Armed with this reaction we were able to go back to the Secretary of State and make a firm offer, subject to the settlement of price and other conditions. So far as the government were concerned, they were sympathetic from the start about what we wanted to do, and we now had the banks behind us as well, subject to an enormous amount of detailed work in preparing the loan agreements and other complicated documents, and – not least – in arranging security for the medium-term loan which would provide the bulk of the purchase price. To give an example of the amount of paperwork and discussion involved, Barclays' original acceptance letter ran to nine closely-typed pages and was based on a scheme which it was hoped would avoid falling foul of Section 54 of the 1948 Companies Act, which came to haunt us over the coming months.

Put simply, Section 54 stopped people buying a company on the security of its own assets. It was designed to prevent fraud, but not designed to deal with the unique situation of employees trying to buy their company from the government with the government's blessing.

It was Section 54 which prevented NFC giving Barclays security on bank loans backed by its properties, and which sent us down tortuous alternative avenues – from which we were eventually rescued by the last-minute appearance of the Seventh Cavalry in the shape of the Companies Act 1981. This measure was before the House as a Bill when our buyout arrangements were nearing completion and it was brought into effect, not entirely coincidentally, in December 1981 just in time for Sections 42–44 to provide a route whereby loans from the banks could be secured against the NFC's properties – though in a rather complicated way in our case.

Back in May–June 1981, however, we had yet to discover the reactions of the rest of our management and all our other employees, the trade unions, the press and the public at large to our proposed buyout. Since the Secretary of State, Norman Fowler, had set 18 June as the day on which he proposed to tell the House of our proposals to buy NFC, we had to ensure that our employees would be informed simultaneously, and we also had to tell the trade unions and the news media.

At very short notice we arranged for the printing of 25,000 copies of an information sheet for every employee, explaining the proposed buyout in simple terms, and had these distributed in sealed bundles to all our branch managers with instructions that they were not to be opened until the afternoon of 18 June, but then every employee was to receive one before close of business. Also at short notice, arrangements were made for senior NFC managers to brief the General Secretaries of the main unions having membership in NFC, and for a press conference in the City of London. Although this had to be set at the normally unpopular time – for the press – of mid-afternoon, we had an excellent turn-out, reflecting the good relations which we had built up with sections of the press over the years through a very open attitude towards the media, and also the lunch meetings with senior financial journalists in 1980 in preparation for the intended flotation. This relationship almost certainly played a part in the next day's press reports which, almost without exception, were enthusiastic; and most of the press remained supportive throughout the whole of the buyout period – and still do today.

The reaction of the trade unions was understandably less enthusiastic: three of the four main unions with members in NFC took the view that, while they opposed denationalization as a matter of policy, our scheme was probably the best way forward in the circumstances. The fourth, and much the biggest, declared its opposition and campaigned against the buyout.

This was a situation we had to live with but meanwhile we had some rapid communicating to do. We had set ourselves a very tight programme for the buyout and, while the complex financial and legal issues were being tackled behind the scenes, we had to discover whether we could interest 24,000 employees and their families and 18,000 pensioners in putting up some money to help us buy the business between us. We started with six large regional meetings at which the leading members of our 'cabal' and myself put out proposals to the rest of our 2,500 managers – with very much the same enthusiastic response which the senior managers had given.

Major Communications Exercise

We now had the task of educating, informing and persuading a large and geographically widespread audience that our novel proposition was in their best interests, against the background of the bankers saying, in effect: 'If you can raise at least four and a quarter million pounds between you, we will lend you the rest to pay the £53.5m. purchase price and the attendant costs.'

Video was the main medium chosen from the mass communications exercise, which was not such an obvious choice in 1981 as it might seem today. The main practical consideration were that the equipment was fairly portable and simple to operate. More significantly, the philosophical choice of video was based on the need to communicate the enthusiasm and commitment of myself and my colleagues in far more locations than we could possibly visit; the fact that visual images were needed to put over a novel and complex message; and the simple fact that the television screen is such a familiar source of information.

There were multiple messages to get across: the basic facts about the buyout proposals, the enthusiasm of the management team, the probable timetable, the nature of shareholding and its rights and obligations, and the variety and scope of NFC's business – since hitherto employees' main interest and knowledge would have centred on their own branch or company. Fortunately the resulting videotape did its job, and so did a second one dealing largely with questions and concerns raised by employees. It was shown just after the prospectus had been issued, and so also dealt with share application.

Backing up the video thrust were printed progress reports, a booklet 'Buying Your Own Company', freephone advice sessions involving senior managers and, of course, the prospectus itself. The latter was obviously a vital piece of communication and, in City terms, ours was a very odd animal indeed. We were determined that, even if all the usual legal and financial information had to be packed in, it would be accompanied by readable, illustrated material in plain English. The fact that over 40 proofs were needed says something for the conservatism of the banking and legal professions and much for our obstinacy. In the end, I think we got it about right and it won considerable acclaim in the financial press for its clarity (Figures 1 and 2).

Waiting for Success

The application lists for buying NFC shares (there were 6,187,500 Ordinary £1 shares on offer at par, payable in full on application) opened on 25 January 1982 and closed on 16 February. Interest-free loans of up to £200 for share purchase were made available to employees, and a target of £4.125m. had been set as the minimum total subscription necessary for success.

At first the response was terrifyingly slow, but it soon became clear that we had a great success on our hands. Applications for over seven million shares were received and, though it went very much against the grain, the applications had to be scaled down and over £800,000 returned.

When people ask me about the relevance of NFC's buyout success for other businesses I always stress the background from which we came as well as the unusual circumstances which gave us a window of opportunity. One of the most important was the fact that NFC never represented more than about 8 per cent of the market it was in, and

Figure 1 How 'A' Ordinary Shares May be Transferred

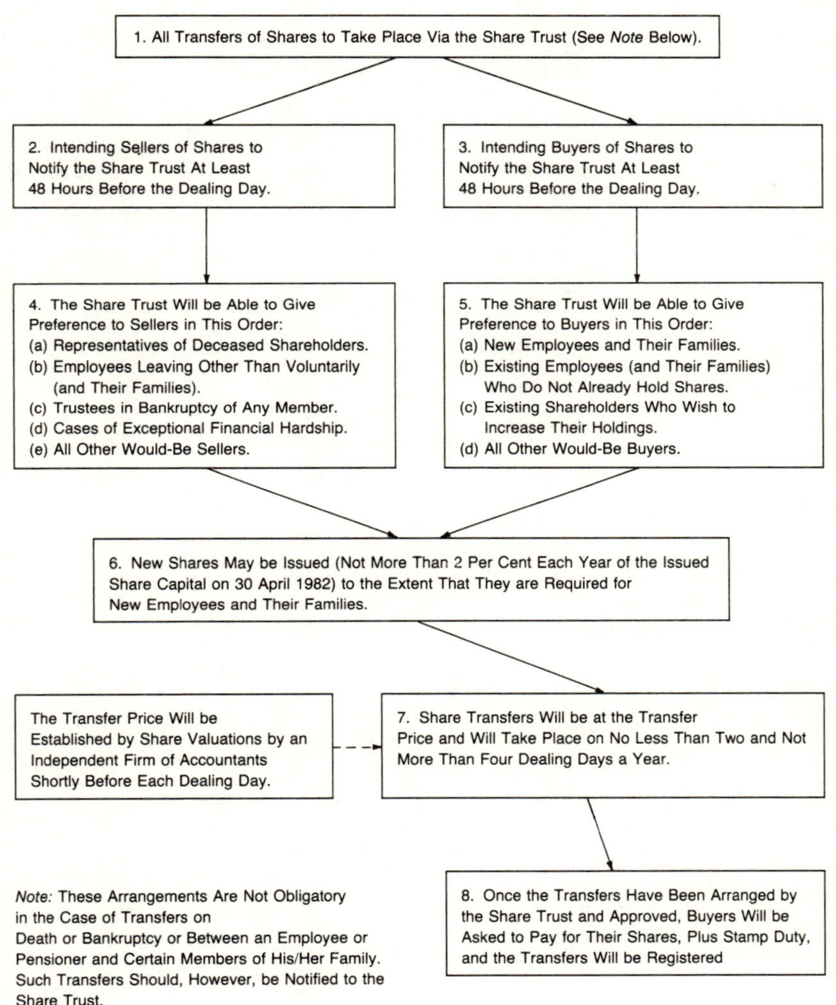

Note: These Arrangements Are Not Obligatory in the Case of Transfers on Death or Bankruptcy or Between an Employee or Pensioner and Certain Members of His/Her Family. Such Transfers Should, However, be Notified to the Share Trust.

Figure 1. An example of how diagrams were used in the 1982 Prospectus to put over complicated concepts—in this case, how the share scheme would work. The Prospectus diagrams were hand-drawn and printed in colour.

Figure 2 How the Purchase Will be Financed

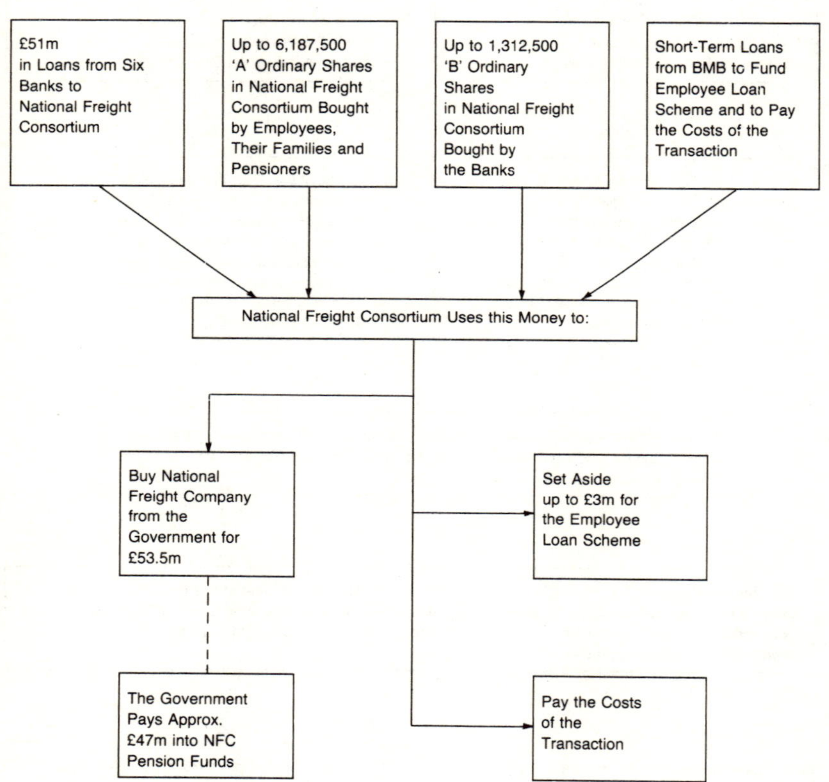

Figure 2. Another diagram from the 1982 Prospectus

this vulnerability to competition – unusual in the public sector – meant that managers were keenly aware of the relationship between productivity and profit. They were also aware of the relationship between effort and reward; some years ago we instituted performance target-setting for the top hundred or so managers in the business, and this process has been extended to managers at all levels and, more recently, to clerical staff. As much as 12.5 per cent of a manager's salary can be dependent upon achieving agreed quality objectives during the year, while one-off bonus payments related to the achievement of cashflow and profit targets can be as much as 30 per cent of salary, depending on the extent to which targets are exceeded. Bonusing is in most cases on a work-unit basis so that many people share in achieving financial targets and benefit thereby. Such a background, I believe, made the acceptance of the risks and corresponding potential of shareholding itself more likely.

Involving the Shareholders

Having bought the business we resolved to involve our new 'owners' in a way that would set NFC apart from other large public companies. Shareholders – most of them employees – have been given opportunties to give management their views. We hold quarterly shareholder meetings chaired by directors in eight regions of the UK; we have used MORI to survey all our shareholders' views about business development, dividend policy, shareholder communication, donation and sponsorship policy, shareholder representation and a host of other issues; we send them a quarterly newsletter about company progress and a range of shareholder matters; we deliberately structure our AGM agenda to promote discussion and the involvement of shareholders in policy decisions; and last year we had a postal ballot of all shareholders to elect a 'shareholder director' to represent their views at Board level. Inevitably many of the questions raised in such forums are more about operating matters than about the wider direction of the business, but that is no bad thing. These people are close to the commercial roots and it can be daunting as Chairman to address an AGM knowing that the shareholders (and we typically have nearly 2,000 at such a meeting) are closely involved and extremely well informed about what actually goes on at the workforce.

At our 1985 AGM we saw industrial democracy very much in action, with voices and votes used very effectively to decide significant issues – and not always in the way the Board intended. I see that as a strength of our policy.

While the shareholders have been quick to use their opportunities to comment – and to vote – they have also proved ready to be guided by the Board and professional management on issues where business experience and judgment are vital. For example, in accepting a modification of our original debt-reduction strategy (involving top priority for paying off our main loan) when we were presented with unprecedented business opportunities requiring investment in new resources.

Broadening the Ownership

One of the subjects on which we have communicated and consulted with shareholders has been the widening of the share ownership among employees, which the Board sees as important. We have had AGM approval for two wider share ownership campaigns – in 1983 and 1985 – with new prospectuses, and these have brought over 6,000 more employee-investors. We have continued to offer an interest-free loan for share purchase by new employees. Our policy is also to keep the 'entry price' low, so as the share value has risen we have split the shares three times to reduce the unit price. Few employee-shareholders have sold out (only 4 per cent last year) and, as Table 3 shows, buyers have been strongly outnumbering sellers in our internal quarterly trading. While this continues we can take the long whether or not to float NFC on the Stock Exchange – which in 1982 we undertook not to do for at least 5 years, and then only with the approval of shareholders in General Meeting*. However, if the strong buying trend was reversed, this would obviously argue cogently in favour of broadening the market beyond NFC itself.

Whatever decision is eventually taken by shareholders, the need to retain the driving power of employee control is obviously going to be a crucial issue. We do not want to destroy the valuable thing we have

* At the time of writing, NFC had not yet obtained a stock exchange listing.

Table 3. On the internal share market, buyers have continued to exceed sellers. This table shows the requests for shares at Dealing Days 3–10, covering 1983 and 1984

Requests for shares at Dealing Days

Dealing Day	Offered	Required	Offered as a % of required
1983— 3	49,548	374,473	13
4	169,184	348,486	48
5	135,815	208,320	65
6	266,042	317,987	84
1984— 7	169,098	524,193	32
8	109,326	421,648	26
9	148,300	300,433	49
10	170,355	327,768	52

NB. Share split after Dealing Day No. 6 discounted.

created and become like any other transport company owned by the City – exchanging one set of faceless shareholders for another. I would also suggest that NFC in its unique new form has earned its exclusion from the political arena.

Meanwhile we have set out strategy for the next 5–10 years after long and deep management discussion and a widespread consultation among shareholders. It is summed up in our new business mission:

> NFC will become a broad based International, Transport, Distribution, Travel and Property Group with a high reputation for service in all its activities. It will retain its commitment to employee control and will use this commitment to expand into associated product areas where service levels are critical. It will have a participative style associated with first-class results-orientated employment packages. It will seek increased employment opportunities and real growth of dividends and share values for its shareholders.

It is a strategy for growth, for high service levels and improved job opportunities, and particularly for a better balanced business. While investing more in UK activities than was ever the case when it was

State-owned, NFC intends to put about a quarter of its investment into overseas activities, mainly in the USA where the returns from transport and distribution activities are about twice those in Britain. In the past NFC has been almost totally dependent on the UK for its income and the intention is to spread the risks and the returns internationally, so that we are no longer so dependent on the comparatively poor-performing home economy. And, while investing heavily in our UK transport and distribution activities and their modern-technology support, we are committed to developing our property interests and expanding our travel business – which is already one of the biggest agencies in Britain.

It is, I think, a measure of the understanding and support of our shareholders that they have accepted this broad view of our future direction. It is also a measure of how employee-shareholders are involved in a business whose ownership they are very conscious of sharing.

17

Brymon Airways – Pre-buyout Turnaround on a Wing and a Prayer

The following case study is based on an edited version of a story by West Country management journalist David Oates that appeared in *Your Business* in 1986.

Charles Stuart, a former senior executive with British Airways, intended his early retirement in the wilds of Devon, fulfilling a long-held ambition to write novels. He bought a remote farm near Tiverton two and a half years ago to escape the high-powered world of civil aviation. In the event, things turned out very differently. Within months of settling in Devon, Stuart received a Mayday to rescue Brymon Airways, a small Plymouth-based airline that was on the brink of liquidation, struggling under the burden of £2.8 million losses.

To all intents and purposes, Brymon looked beyond salvation and most people would have expected it to join the ranks of small business failures in a market dominated by the major airlines. Stuart, a dogged Scotsman who had behind him the invaluable experience of having been marketing director for British European Airways for many years before it merged with BOAC, decided, however, to shelve his early retirement plans and rise to the challenge. Through a combination of astute marketing and professional management, he slowly pulled Brymon back from the abyss of extinction. By the end of last year (1985), he had piloted it back to the break-even point of a turnover of £9 million.

Stuart has not only ensured Brymon's survival. He has brought it to the point where it is the only airline in the country that is likely to be able to take full advantage of the projected £15 million London City airport project planned as part of the Docklands redevelopment scheme. The short-take-off-and-land (STOL) airport will bring business travellers to within a 20-minute taxi ride of the City of London.

Brymon is the only British airline with operational experience of the super-quiet De Havilland Dash–7 aircraft, which alone meets the stringent requirements for an airport so close to the heart of one of the most densely populated cities in the world. If STOLport works for London, there is no reason why the concept should not be adopted by other cities all over Europe. Brymon, therefore, stands poised to cash in on an aviation revolution.

An extraordinary role was played by Canadian planemakers De Havilland in Brymon's remarkable transformation. When the airline stood on the brink of disaster, it was expected that De Havilland would foreclose on its assets – the fleet of aircraft Brymon had not yet paid for – and take the safest and most economical route out of its involvement with the airline. Instead, De Havilland took the daring gamble of converting from a major creditor to a majority shareholder by opting for a 75 per cent stake in Brymon. It made it clear at the time, however, that this was only to be a temporary measure.

When by the middle of last year (1985), it was apparent that Brymon was out of the storm, rumours were rife that several well-known airlines and consortia were bidding to take over De Havilland's stake. As Brymon's chairman and chief executive, Stuart had the task of appraising the bids, but surreptitiously he was putting together a deal of his own behind the scenes. At the end of last year (1985), he revealed one of the best-kept secrets in the aviation business – that he and his executive board had successfully taken financial control in a £10-million management buyout. It was a triple-package deal, involving loans raised against the value of the airline's assets, personal equity from the executives, and a small equity stake by British Airways.

It seemed only fitting to Stuart that the new management team he had recruited to inject professionalism into the airline and which had worked so tirelessly to bring about the airline's reconstruction should end up with the majority shareholding. He now plans to offer a small proportion of the shares to the airline's 210 employees and he will shortly be drawing up a profit-sharing scheme.

A vital element in Stuart's successful bid was the backing from British Airways. British Airways has taken a 14 per cent trading investment, which gives it only limited voting rights. Brymon's trump hand with STOLport was undoubtedly one of the enticements for BA, but Stuart sees it as more than that. He describes BA's support as 'a kind of seal of good housekeeping' accolade.

'If British Airways has confidence in us, we should have confidence in ourselves', he stresses in his Plymouth airport office, which has an enormous window overlooking the runway. Stuart's soft-spoken words are periodically drowned by the arrival of an aircraft which taxis down the runway before spilling out another load of executive passengers clutching briefcases. Brymon now carries three times as many passengers on its scheduled Plymouth to Heathrow route as it did in 1981. The airport, which is perched on a hill overlooking Plymouth and is prone to foggy weather that drifts in from the coast, is also run by Brymon, and upgrading its inadequate facilities was another headache Stuart took on when he agreed to mastermind Brymon's recovery.

The relief at having pulled off the buyout deal is evident on Stuart's face. He smiles a lot more than he used to and his eyes light up when discussing the airline's future prospects. He spent months on detailed negotiations, confidently leaving the day-to-day running of the airline in the hands of his executive board.

He is convinced that Brymon's more professional approach has not gone unnoticed by British Airways.

> BA's modest share is out of all proportion to its importance. In effect, British Airways is saying that we are well-managed, well-run and have good potential prospects for regional development. It is also saying that we merit its interest. For BA to say that about an airline with only five aircraft in the winter and six aircraft in the summer is an incredible achievement.

If the London Docklands STOLport project gets off the ground as planned by the middle of 1987, however, Stuart envisages Brymon trebling its fleet of aircraft. The small airline will then have to make investments that will probably quadruple its current £12 million asset base. To prepare itself for this major leap forward, Brymon is planning a flotation on the USM some time this year (1986).

In coping with such rapid expansion, it is comforting for Brymon to have the support of BA, but 57–year-old Stuart stresses that it is 'a totally hands-off relationship'. He adds, picking his words carefully:

> British Airways is clear that our strategic aims are complementary to theirs. They are looking for regional airlines that can make a go of it, can be both profitable in their own right and complementary to British Airways' own international market developments.
>
> British Airways believes that by investing in us it has an opportunity to keep an eye on what we're doing, so that as we get stronger and flourish and become more profitable they can say whether the new markets they wish to open up are appropriate for us to open up. In our turn, we can look at those markets and say whether we want to do it.

Although Stuart underlines Brymon's independence, he nevertheless acknowledges BA's crucial contribution in a close-run fight to win control of the airline. At one time 20 different airlines and consortia were courting Brymon and the final short-list of around six contenders meant that Stuart's bid was by no means a foregone conclusion. He confesses:

> We just scraped in above the minimum selling price. Every bit of the negotiation was a problem and I didn't know we had succeeded until I received De Havilland's telegram. I think it was important to De Havilland that they should sell to someone who would keep Brymon on the same track it has been going.

Hard fights are nothing new to Stuart. Few would have fancied the airline's chances of survival when he took over the hot seat in October 1983. In the first few months, so many problems were hitting him at once he hardly dared open his post or answer the telephone. His one piece of good fortune in facing an otherwise totally bleak picture was De Havilland's willingness to give Brymon the benefit of the doubt.

> It's difficult to imagine how the airline could have survived if De Havilland hadn't been prepared to stick by us. They would have made more money realizing their assets. Most major creditors might well have pulled out,

> but they decided to put up with the anguish of continuing to be involved in the management of the airline.

The anguish soon turned to relief, however, as Stuart moved swiftly to take charge of a rapidly deteriorating situation. He put into effect professional management techniques, partly drawn from his 15 years experience with BEA and British Airways, and put in tight managerial and operational controls.

He brought in a virtually new top team of professional managers and gave everyone job descriptions so that they all knew what was expected of them. His masterplan for financial reconstruction was to carry the same number of passengers with one less aircraft. By balancing schedules and maximizing resources, the airline was soon achieving levels of business that were 10 points above its budgeted load factor, something Stuart looks back on as 'incredible'. He concentrated almost entirely on executive passengers, a more lucrative and reliable market, eschewing the more fickle tourist trade.

As Brymon steadily pulled out of its nosedive, however, it flew into another heavy storm cloud. Sterling was falling dramatically against the dollar and it became even more imperative to keep a tight control of the airline's finances. All Brymon's major costs are in dollars, while it has practically no dollar income. 'It was the superior-to-budget performance on cost control that enabled us to absorb the higher dollar costs without any dollar income', observes Stuart with satisfaction.

Comparing the way the airline operates today with its former operational style, Stuart adds:

> To me, it's the difference between running a pioneering airline (where, in effect, the captains are running it for you and you have a few small planes buzzing about happily without a lot of thought for tomorrow and no ambition) and a professional airline that is hoping to go international on the most important international routes in Europe for probably the most sensitive and influential customers an airline can have at the moment.
>
> That to me symbolizes our approaching maturity. We shall have this intellectual discipline for our approach to London City STOLport. I am confident now that we have, perhaps just in time, reached the point where the expansion we shall need to go through can be accommodated without tearing us apart.

Stuart is particularly proud of the strength of the management team he has built up.

> The airline now has an executive board comprising departmental heads who are professional managers of their departments, trained for the job, who understand their interlinking relationships with one another. We meet regularly once a week to survey the course of the business. It now runs quite smoothly with a sense of professional style about it. We've worked our way through to a team in which there is a good rapport between all the people who sit around my table and they're all competent people in their own right.'

Only Harry Gee, fleet operations manager, has survived from the airline's previous era. One of the professionals Stuart brought in was John Jones, as commercial manager, from Laker Airways. Jones is not part of the buyout group, however. He accepted a position at Dan Air before it was known that Stuart's bid had been approved by De Havilland.

Stuart has such faith in his executive team that he will be looking for a successor as chief executive in the next six months. He already held a 5 per cent stake in Brymon when it was under De Havilland's control. His stake in the buyout has altered his position very little and he sees no reason why the change of ownership should affect his decision to take a back seat now that Brymon appears to be on a safe course.

He nevertheless plans to remain as a non-executive chairman and to play a key role in preparing Brymon for its dominant part in the STOLport project. Brymon intends to open its services from the Docklands airport in 1987 with eight destinations – five on the Continent and three in the UK.

Stuart has served notice, however, that Brymon is not prepared to wait indefinitely for the STOLport project to become operational. He has alternative plans to develop regional air services with the more advanced 36-seater Dash–8, whether or not STOLport goes ahead. Inevitably the application by construction giant Mowlem to build STOLport has gone through a protracted inquiry procedure, with objectors claiming it will be too noisy and dangerous.

When the go-ahead was finally given, the De Havilland Dash–7 was the only plane at the starting gate that could meet the stringent operational constraints. Brymon has had ideal short-take-off-and-land experience in ferrying oil men to Unst in Scotland en route to the North Sea oil fields. Unst is the northernmost airport in Britain with an extremely short runway. 'If the international operation develops out of London, I would like as a non-executive chairman, to retain the strategic interest of shepherding that along, because it is my principal contribution. I know how to do it', says Stuart.

He has no qualms about handing over the reins to a new chief executive. He is certain the executive board can manage 'the airline they have created'. He points out that for much of 1985, he had effectively been operating as a non-executive chairman. Most of his time was devoted to putting the buyout deal together and dealing with bids from other contendors. During that time, he observes, his executive board had to run the airline through some of the worst weather conditions for a long time.

> We actually had a summer with the weather record of winter, which imposed enormous disproportionate delays and diversions of the kind we don't normally expect. It was an enormous reassurance to me that the executive board handled that with the minimum of disruption to passengers.
>
> They've run a good airline in my absence. It is a remarkable testimony to them. It is a totally different airline from the one I came to in October 1983.

18

M.4 Data – The Buyout at Speed

The following case study, again by West Country management journalist David Oates, appeared in *Your Business* in 1987.

Few buyouts have been formed so quickly and with such ease as M.4 Data. The Surrey-based company came into existence as a result of a buyout of Thorn EMI's £10 million computer drive business, part of the group's Datatech division.

Once it was decided to go ahead with the buyout last summer (1986), it took barely three weeks to get the new company on the road. In order to move that fast, 3i (Investors In Industry) initially underwrote the entire £4.5 million deal through its 'hands-on' ventures division, syndicating it out, after M.4 had been established, to other venture capital groups. These include some of the leading UK financial institutions such as Citicorp Venture Capital, Charterhouse Japhet and ECI (Equity Capital for Industry).

Dr Duke Ebenezer, M.4 Data's chief executive, felt there were compelling arguments to move at such incredible speed. In an office of M.4 Data's R&D laboratories at Wookey Hole in Somerset he recalls the situation:

> Usually these things take six months. My co-founders, David Huntingdon, Frank Cowley and myself, together with our backers 3i Ventures, set ourselves deadlines which gave us literally about three weeks. If we had not met the deadlines we set ourselves together with Thorn EMI the whole deal would have been off, because the customers would have begun to hear what was going on and might well have lost confidence in us. Thorn EMI was also anxious not to cause confusion among employees in other divisions.

Completing the deal in such a short time-span meant working at a furious intensity for all concerned. When it was still part of Thorn EMI, the computer drive business had built up a solid customer base of such blue-chip companies as Hewlett Packard, Computer Vision and Gould in the USA and ICL in the UK. But 3i Ventures was still determined to undertake a thorough analysis of the proposed new company's future plans. Ebenezer says:

> Whilst they understood the market place we were in, they looked at everything in great detail. They worked on it day and night. They looked at our financial records, our future plans, precisely how we were going to tackle the market place in Europe, the US and the rest of the world, what kind of new products we were going to design and how we were going to compete against the Americans and Japanese technically. All these commercial aspects were analysed with due diligence, even though it was done within a very short time scale.

Thorn EMI, too, 'bent over backwards', as Ebenezer puts it, to conclude the buyout swiftly. For example, there was insufficient time to transfer the sales and marketing operations in the US and West Germany to M.4 Data before the deal was struck. 'These outlets continued to operate under Thorn EMI for several months under an agency agreement. We paid them agency fees and they continued to trade on our behalf. Our customers were informed of what was going on and they were not affected in any way', explains Ebenezer. 'Indeed', he added, 'Thorn EMI Datatech management and employees continue to assist us in many ways.'

The swift transition already seems to be paying dividends for M.4 Data. Although it is early days, the company is ahead of its turnover target in excess of £10 million for its first trading year and the number of employees has increased from 100 to 150 in six months.

Ebenezer and his top management team took the decision to go for a buyout at a time when Thorn EMI was re-appraising its business strategy. The leading electronics group was determined to concentrate on its mainline products. Although it was prepared to continue to support the tape drive business, it was unlikely to make the sort of investments Ebenezer felt were needed to see the business grow at a healthy rate.

As part of Thorn EMI, the business had made an aggressive attack on the high-technology end of the market. It had grown from an annual turnover of a few hundred thousand pounds to one of several million pounds in five years. But Ebenezer found the business uncomfortably lodged between two competing forces in the international market place. On one side were the large American specialist companies with turnovers of hundreds of millions of dollars. 'Then there's the competition from the entrepreneurial start-up company, which of course is very responsive, innovative and gets its products to market on time', elaborates Ebenezer. 'We fitted into neither a specialist company that had large revenues nor a start-up company, which is very much more responsive'.

M.4 Data, as a buyout, had some distinct advantages over the conventional start-up company, however. Not the least of these was ongoing contracts with some blue-chip customers. As Ebenezer points out:

> These are long-term contracts with original equipment manufacturers – computer manufacturers who buy the products we make and integrate them into their systems before selling on to the end-user. It's a very good ongoing business. You don't have to sell each product you make to different end-users. We also had four world firsts in our product range. So we had an excellent pedigree.

Ebenezer's first and only choice to fund the buyout was 3i Ventures, because some ex-colleagues had previously started a company in Scotland which is now turning over £100 million with support from 3i. 'We also knew people in 3i who had particular experience of this kind of industry. In fact, one of the directors of 3i was the ex-vice-president of one of our biggest competitors in California', says Ebenezer with a wry smile.

In addition to the £4.5 million put up by 3i, M.4 Data also obtained a £1.5 million loan facility from the Bank of Scotland, which it has so far not needed to draw on. The original £4.5 million has now been syndicated among several leading venture capital groups, including Citicorp Venture Capital, Charterhouse Japhet and Equity capital for Industry (ECI).

Ebenezer admits that M.4 Data misses some of the back-up facilities it enjoyed as part of the Thorn EMI group, including use of the corporate patents office. But wherever it is lacking in internal expertise it has appointed outside agents. On the whole, being an independent company offers singular advantages and the switch-over has not been as demanding as it might have been.

> Whilst we were part of Thorn EMI, the company had a policy of making each business totally accountable and self-sufficient. We were encouraged for commercial reasons to behave like a small company that had to support itself. What has changed is the motivation, which is now there throughout the company. The results are plain to see. All our employees will take part in a profit-sharing scheme, provided we meet the first-year objectives.

Ebenezer faces the future with confidence: 'With greater flexibility, we shall become exactly attuned to the design, quality and reliability needs of the major computer companies. We shall continue to generate world-beating designs.'

19

Mecca Leisure Group – A Classic Diversification Buyout

Most people think of Mecca as a relatively modern company, born of the bingo boom. In reality, however, the company has a much longer history and a much wider range of activities. Founded in 1884 to sell coffee grinding machinery, it became a public company 14 years later, at which time it began to establish a successful chain of coffee houses within the City of London. Gradually expanding into entertainment and other forms of catering, it spread into the provinces until, by the 1950s, it was running dance halls across the country.

In 1961 (coincidentally the year that the present chairman, Michael Guthrie, joined) Mecca brought an American craze – bingo – into the UK. It was a runaway success, with weekly audiences of 15 million at its peak. Even now, when the craze is long past, weekly audiences number about 5 million and are increasing. Mecca invested some of its income in diversifications into casinos and bookmaking. It also included among its more glamorous activities the Miss World competition.

For Grand Metropolitan Hotels, Mecca was an obvious fit in its strategy for the 1970s. GrandMet's Maxwell Joseph acquired the company in 1970 and absorbed it into the group to the extent that the gambling activities were separated from Mecca organizationally in 1979. Warner Holidays, another GrandMet takeover, was brought under Mecca's management in 1983 as a logical leisure group fit. However, partly because of Mecca's share structure (the absorption of Clubman's Club in 1969 had left a block of Mecca shares in the hands of the Clubman's founders), it retained a clear identity within the group as part of the consumer services division, which also included Berni Inns and the Host chain of public houses, GrandMet's management style also helped, with its stress on operational autonomy.

Being part of a larger group has its advantages, but it had one major disadvantage – Mecca was prevented from pursuing opportunities in areas where it had key expertise. 'We had been constrained in expansion terms', says finance director, Jeremy Long. 'Catering and restaurants are an area we have always been in, from the company's early days. But GrandMet saw this as the metier of its pub divisions.'

By the mid-1980s, GrandMet's grand strategy was changing. Rapid expansion in the United States and in less mature markets led to a new focus of activities. Companies that did not fit the new focus, or were too demanding of top management attention for their size, were to be disposed of. The northern division of Express Dairies was one of the first major divestments, followed by Pinkerton Tobacco in the United States. Then, as the strategy faltered and was given an extra impetus, a top-level strategy meeting in early 1985 pinpointed Mecca as a divestment target. As *Financial Weekly* commented: 'Mecca was deemed to be insufficiently large and too mature to rank as a main leg for the group.' A lesser, but still influential, consideration, probably was that Mecca had a high public profile, something that GrandMet was never really comfortable with.

No one suggested that Mecca was not a viable and successful operation. It had a strong asset base, and profits had risen from £4.5 million in 1982 to £7.4 million in 1984 and reached £9.5 million in 1985. Turnover in 1984 was £114 million, rising to £124 million in 1985.

The decision hit the Mecca top managers hard. 'My first reaction was a very human one', Guthrie told *Money Management*. 'It was hard to believe that after all our work in making the company a success, they wanted to sell.' Long recalls:

> In May 1985, Michael Guthrie and I were informed by GrandMet that the business was to be sold and that our personal positions would be protected. We could transfer within GrandMet or, if we decided to quit, our severance terms would be met. GrandMet wanted our help to sell the company. We took legal advice about our contracts and it was our

solicitors, Herbert Oppenheimer, Nathan and Vandyk who suggested that we should consider buying the company out ourselves.

Guthrie and Long formed a buyout team with the heads of Mecca's two main divisions and took on Deloitte, Haskins and Sells as financial advisers. 'About a month later, at a meeting with GrandMet, we said: "Would you consider the managers as one of the potential buyers?" ' GrandMet agreed, but refused to give the managers any preferential treatment. Quite the contrary, in fact; Guthrie and his colleagues were forbidden to talk about their bid to the press, nor could they approach financial institutions overtly to put together a bid package. 'We were able to talk to them, but not to divulge any business information', says Long.

With the help of Deloittes, Guthrie and his colleagues started looking for a financial backer. They interviewed a number of potential lead investors, looking for a combination of professionalism and compatibility, and finally selected Samuel Montagu. Given that Mecca had all the hallmarks of an ideal buyout, the managers insisted that the merchant banks provide their support and advice on a 'no deal; no fee' basis.

Some time after the discussions with GrandMet, the news that the division was for sale spread around the City and it rapidly became clear that there would be other bidders. When it was formally announced in October that a number of parties, including the top managers, were interested in buying Mecca, that attracted yet further attention. The press comment on the forthcoming sale inevitably compared and contrasted the chances of the various known or suspected bidders. Guthrie's agreement not to speak to the press about the buyout bid meant that he was unable to put his case publicly and that what appeared in print was wildly inaccurate. He later told *Financial Weekly:* 'It was like being in a contested bid situation with your hands tied behind your back'. The press articles suggested that the management was offering only half the expected bid price of £100 million and that it had had great difficulty in raising the cash to offer even that amount. Montagu, which felt its reputation was on the line, informed GrandMet that it was going to explain the true situation and did so. It revealed why the managers had been unable to comment and pointed out potential problems with the rival Rank bid – among them, the possibility of reference to the Monopolies Commission.

The scene was rapidly being set for an auction in which the managers would be squeezed out of the running. In the event, however, GrandMet decided it preferred the buyout terms to those offered by the Rank Organization and at least one other bidder. 'It was in the final stages of the negotiations that they realized our bid was preferable', says Long. The reasons were several. First and perhaps most importantly, GrandMet was able to insist that the buyout team agree to continue to maintain the 'tied house' arrangement with Watneys for all its existing licensed leisure premises, for ten years. Secondly, the warranties that would be demanded from the buyout team (who knew the business and its liabilities inside out) would be fewer and less stringent than would be the case with a third party purchaser. The buyout team was more malleable, in the sense that it was in a difficult position when it came to negotiating. GrandMet shrewdly insisted that negotiations must be between the group and the Mecca managers, a move that put considerable pressure on them. As Long said:

> The buyout was emotionally very draining. It turned the boss/subordinate relationship on its head. You have to negotiate very hard with people who have been (and at that stage still were) your bosses. I'd been at Mecca for eight years; the other three 20–plus years each. So there was a lot of loyalty towards the company from everyone in the buyout team.

A third reason was that pressure was now being put on GrandMet by the press to be seen to deal fairly with its managers. Having been given an insight into why the managers had been so unhelpful over information on the terms of the buyout bid, the press now became strong supporters and made it clear that, if GrandMet accepted anything short of a substantially better offer from an outsider, it would be seen as selling a loyal management down the river. GrandMet's management, to be fair, saw the situation in much the same light, not least because most of the bidders were real or potential competitors.

The downside of the buyout was that the buyout team could not offer cash on the nail, whereas the other bidders could. So GrandMet put even further pressure on the buyout team, which had by now increased its offer from £90 million to £95 million against a bid from Rank which was later estimated by observers to have been £100 million. Guthrie and his colleagues had two days in which to gain agreement from Montagu to underwrite both the equity and the loan funding. Even given that the loan funding made up less than 60 per cent of the total, it was a major commitment for Montagu to make. 'That GrandMet was determined to get a full price didn't surprise me; but the terms they gave us did', recalls Long.

In the event, Montagu persuaded the Royal Bank of Scotland to shoulder half the loan risk and accepted the other half itself. The fact that the merchant bank and the clearing bank did so reflects the health of the company and the solidity of its asset base. In particular, Mecca's property was conservatively estimated at £73 million in September 1985. Most of the property was owned; most of the rest had long leases. Some of the sites have significant development potential.

Samuel Montagu had constructed an arrangement that would give the four principals 10 per cent of the equity for £500,000. In addition, there was to be an option of a further 5 per cent for 360 senior and general managers, conditional upon fulfilling the first year's profit projections. The options can be exercised at any time over a three to seven year period. 'Under GrandMet there was a share option scheme', says Long, 'but it applied to only some people in Mecca. Overnight we took the number of people involved in this way to cover all the key people, including all branch managers.' The structure of the financing was £40.5 million in equity, the rest as loans.

'We spent the three weeks between the end of November and shortly before Christmas raising the money', says Long. The loan funding was eventually sold down to five banks and the equity dispersed through a series of presentations across the country, in London, Manchester, Edinburgh and Glasgow. 'We finally completed on the 20th of December.'

One of the promises made to the institutions was that Mecca would float within two years and a date of August 1987 was set. In the event, as it became clear that the profit target figure would be reached, the company returned to the Stock Exchange in August 1986. As Long explained:

> We had been told we would get better terms if we waited, but we had other reasons for going sooner. In particular, we were conscious that we had spent five years building up a structure and a management team that could increase the business. We'd seen so many buyouts go through a long initial period of austerity to cope with their debt. But we didn't want to lose momentum or go into reverse, because we could lose too

> many good people at that stage. So we began planning the flotation within a fortnight of the buyout. The date for the flotation was two weeks after our year end, so we had to float on an estimate of our outgoing year. We estimated – accurately as it proved – a level of trading profit 42 per cent up on the previous year, at £13.6 million. This was above the figures in the buyout document.

Between the buyout and the flotation, in February 1986, the company turned half of its short-term debt into a 20-year debenture – almost equivalent to a preference share, in its practical effect. It had given an undertaking, during the negotiations with the bankers, to do so within twelve months. This reduced the banks' risk exposure and made it easier to sell the deal. While the level of gearing stayed at around 35 per cent, loan capital repayments became much less of a burden on current operations.

Six months after the flotation, Mecca is pushing for rapid growth. According to Long:

> We are keen to expand our core businesses. But we will supplement organic growth by buying more businesses. We will move laterally into areas where our skills can be used, such as hotels. With the Warner holiday centres we already operate what is in many respects an all year round country club business, so this would be a natural expansion.

Released from the constraints of being part of the larger group – not least the difficulty of presenting a glamorous, bright-lights public image in an organization that traditionally hides its light – Mecca has tapped the enthusiasm of its key staff. 'You only realize afterwards', Guthrie was quoted as saying, 'how anaesthetized and frustrated you've been.' And elsewhere: 'My attitude towards business is no different post-buyout, but it gives me the ability to move much faster in the market place. Mecca is rapidly returning to being an entrepreneurial company.'

Appendix 1: Glossary

ASSET VALUE — An estimate of the realizable value of the company's assets after deducting the known liabilities and dividing the result amongst the equity shareholders. In a takeover, the declared asset value of a company's shares is usually greater than their market price. The 'break-up' value is often more relevant and this is a notional figure gained by assuming the break-up of the company and dividing the estimated proceeds by the number of shares.

BRIDGE-FINANCING — Loans required in the period between the buyout and when the company goes public.

DEBENTURES

DEBENTURE — A document outlining the terms of a loan. It is normally, though not always, secured on the company's assets.

UNSECURED DEBENTURES — Debt acknowledgement without security.

SECURED DEBENTURES — A charge taken on the company's assets, either a fixed charge on a particular asset or a floating charge placed on total assets.

REGISTERED DEBENTURES — In the name of a registered holder and able to be exchanged like shares.

BEARER DEBENTURES — Payable to the bearer, they are negotiable instruments transferable by delivery, similar to share warrants.

CONVERTIBLE DEBENTURES — Holders can change their debentures for shares.

REDEEMABLE DEBENTURES — The company is bound to repay the nominal amount at a fixed date, upon demand, or periodically.

PERPETUAL OR REDEEMABLE DEBENTURES — The amount is only repayable through company liquidation or a breach of debenture conditions.

SERIES OF DEBENTURES — Are issued to a number of lenders in a series and are usually ranked equally.

DEBENTURE STOCK — Where multiple loans are grouped into one composite debt and each contributor holds a debenture stock certificate to the value of his contribution. This simplifies the transfer of part of a holding.

DEPRECIATION — In practice, this is the amount allocated from each year's profits to cover the writing off of fixed assets.

DILAPIDATION LIABILITIES — The liability of a long-term tenant to compensate the landlord upon the termination of the lease for any deterioration of the property.

DIVIDENDS — The amount of a company's profit paid to shareholders at the discretion of the directors or the annual general meeting. Dividends are stated as a percentage of the nominal value of the share. All dividends are subject to tax which is paid by the company before distribution.

EARNINGS — The amount available to the company to distribute among its ordinary shareholders.

HIVE DOWNS — Where the parent company transfers certain assets to a newly created subsidiary on loan account. This is then purchased by the buyout group for a nominal consideration, and it refinances the loan due to the parent company.

LEAD INVESTOR — The backer with the largest stake in the company who usually plays an active role in the company's development.

LEVERAGED BUYOUTS — Involve taking on non-equity liabilities such as loans and extended credit arrangements to fund the acquisition of the company.

LIQUID ASSETS — Assets in cash or which can be readily converted into cash.

LOAN CAPITAL — Capital which ranks as fixed period debt, the most common form of which are debentures.

MARKET VALUATION — The amount a company's share capital would realize if sold in a completely free market.

PRICE EARNINGS RATIO — Market price per ordinary share divided by earnings per ordinary share after tax. It indicates the market value placed on the expectation of future earnings, that is, the amount of time needed to cover the price paid for the share, out of profits at the current rate.

RATCHETS — Incentive conditions built into the loan to give equity rewards if profits rise above target, or penalties if this is not achieved.

SECOND ROUND FINANCING — Additional injection of capital when the company is up and running but needs extra funds to build on the base or to bring new projects to completion.

SHARES

CUMULATIVE PREFERENCE SHARES — Holders have preferential rights as to dividend and capital, and rank equally with the other Ordinary holders. The voting rights are restricted, but the holders can convert their shares into Ordinary shares at any time.

ORDINARY SHARES — Entitle the holder to share in profits after prior demands such as loan interest or preference dividends have been met.

PREFERENCE SHARES — Entitle the holders to a fixed dividend before anything is paid to holders of Ordinary shares, but the holders have extremely limited voting rights.

REDEEMABLE SHARES — Preference shares which are redeemable at the option of either the company or the shareholder.

RIGHTS ISSUE — When additional shares in the company are offered to existing shareholders in proportion to their holdings, at a price usually lower than it would be in the open market.

SYNDICATED INVESTMENT — Divided between several backers for investments too large, too complex or too risky to be taken on by a single buyer.

WARRANTY — A statement in a contract which protects the buyer if the seller has not fulfilled it. For example, if the seller claims to have assets which do not appear after the buyout, or if there are undeclared liabilities, the buyer may be able to claim damages, using the warranty as proof.

YIELD BASIS — The return which the dividend gives expressed as a percentage of the current market price of the shares.

Appendix 2: Contacts: Investors

Bank of Scotland, 38 Threadneedle Street, London, EC2P 2EH.
Tel: 01–628–8060
Contact: Colin Matthew (Senior Manager)

Bankers Trust International Ltd, Dashwood House, 69 Old Broad Street, London, EC2P 3EE.
Tel: 01–726–4141
Contact: Gordon Bonnyman

Barclays Development Capital Ltd, Pickfords Wharf, Clink St, London, SE1 9DG.
Tel: 01–407–2389
Contact: Michael Cumming

British Linen Bank, 55 Bishopsgate, London, EC2.
Tel: 01–588–7911
Contacts: Ian Macpherson, Douglas Anderson

Candover Investments, Cedric House, 8–9 East Harding Street, London, EC4A 3AS.
Tel: 01–583–5090
Contact: Roger Brooke

Charterhouse Developments, 6 New Bridge Street, London, EC4V 6SH.
Tel: 01–248–4000

CIN Industrial Investments, P.O. Box 10, London, SW1X 7AD.
Tel: 01–245–6911
Contact: D. Prosser

Citicorp Venture Capital, 2, Savoy Court, London, WC2R 0E2.
Tel: 01–240–1222
Contact: Charles Gonfzor

County Bank Ltd, 11 Old Broad Street, London, EC2N 1BR.
Tel: 01–638–6000
Contacts: C.R. Bloomfield, A. Davison

Development Capital Group Ltd, 44 Baker Street, London, W1.
Tel: 01–935–2731
Contact: N. Falkner

Electra Investment Trust plc, Electra House, Temple Place, London, WC2R 3HP.
Tel: 01–836–7766
Contact: M. Stoddart

Equity Capital for Industry, Leith House, 47/57 Gresham Street, London, EC2V 7EH.
Tel: 01–606–8513
Contact: J. A. Lorenz

First National Bank of Boston, 5 Cheapside, London, EC2P 2DE.
Tel: 01–236–2388

Foreign & Colonial Investment Trust plc, 1 Laurence Pountney Hill, London, EC4R 0BA.
Tel: 01–623–4680
Contact: James Nelson

Fountain Development Capital Fund, 100 Wood Street, London, EC2P 2AJ.
Tel: 01–628–8011
Contacts: David Osborne, Anthony Wheaton

Gresham Trust Ltd, Barrington House, Gresham Street, London, EC2.
Tel: 01–606–6474
Contact: P. Smaill

Hill Samuel, 100 Wood Street, London, EC2P 2AJ.
Tel: 01–628–8011
Contacts: Billy Chambers, Colin Ansell

Investors in Industry, 91 Waterloo Road, London, SE1 8XP.
Tel: 01–928–7822
Contacts: Richard Connell, John Kingston

Lloyds Merchant Bank Ltd, 40–66 Queen Victoria Street, London, EC4P 4EL.
Tel: 01–248–2244.
Contact: Ron Hollidge

Manufacturers Hanover Trust Co., 7 Princes Street, London, EC2P 2LR.
Tel: 01–600–5666

Midland Equity Group, Watling Court, 47–53 Cannon Street, London, EC4M 5SQ.
Tel: 01–638–8861

Midland Montagu Ventures Ltd, Norfolk House, 3, Laurence Pountney Hill, London, EC4R 0BP.
Tel: 01–260–8000
Contact: Dr Hugh de Quervain (Managing Director)

Laurie Milbank, 72 Basinghall Street, London, EC2.
Tel: 01–606–6622

G.T.A.W. Horton, Minster Trust, Minster House, 12 Arthur Street, London, EC4R 9BH.
Tel: 01–623–1050

Samuel Montagu, 114 Old Broad Street, London, EC2P 2HY.
Tel: 01–588–6464

Morgan Grenfell Asset Management, 23 Great Winchester Street, London, EC2P 2AX.
Tel: 01–588–4545

Morgan Guaranty Ltd, 83, Pall Mall, London, SW1Y 7ES.
Tel: 01–930–9444

National Westminster, County Development Capital, Drapers Garden, 12, Frogmorton Avenue, London, EC2P 2ES.
Tel: 01–382–1000
Contact: Robert Drummond

PIC Capital Group, 51, Bow Lane, London, EC4M 9HB.
Tel: 01–283–8122
Contact: Martin Imm

Prudential Venture Managers, 142 Holborn Bars, London, EC1N 2NH.
Tel: 01–404–5611
Contacts: Paul Brooks, Michael Geary

Philips & Drew Development Capital, Triton Court, 14 Finsbury Square, London, EC2A 1BR.
Tel: 01–628–6366
Contact: Ian Hawkins

Scandinavian Bank Ltd, Scandinavian House, 2–6 Cannon Street, London, EC4M 6XX.
Tel: 01–236–6090
Contact: Simon Dawes

Schroder Venture, The Schroder Group, Regina House, 5, Queen St, London, EC4 N15P.
Tel: 01–382–6000
Contact: Jon Moulton

Scimitar Development Capital Ltd, 33–36, Gracechurch St, London, EC3V 0AX.
Tel: 01–623–8711
Contact: Richard Arthur

Scottish Development Agency, 120 Bothwell Street, Glasgow, GW2.
Tel: 041–248–2700
Contact: John Gow (Investment Manager)

Security Pacific Eurofinance UK Ltd, The Adelphi, John Adam St, London, WC2N 6HP.
Tel: 01–930–7902
Contact: Stephen Walton

Singer & Friedlander Ltd, 206, Derby Road, Nottingham, NG7 1NQ.
Tel: 0602 419721

S. G. Warburg, 30 Gresham Street, London, EC2P 2EB.
Tel: 01–600–4555

Appendix 3: Contacts: Advisers

Base International, Midsummer House, 443 Midsummer Boulevard, Central Milton Keynes, MK9 3BN.
Tel: 0908 664315
Contact: Anthony Lunch

Blackstone, Franks, Smith & Co., 388/396 Oxford Street, London, W1N 9HE.
Tel: 01–491–4924
Contact: L. R. Blackstone

County Securities, 1 Finsbury Square, London, EC2.
Tel: 01–588–2525
Contact: Peter St. George

Deloitte Haskins & Sells, 128 Queen Victoria Street, London, EC4.
Tel: 01–248–3913
Contact: Geoffrey Westmore

Granville & Co. Ltd, 8 Lovat Lane, London, EC3R 8BP.
Tel: 01–621–1212
Contact: C. Moy

Guidehouse Ltd, Vestry House, Greyfriars Passage, Newgate Street, London, EC1A 7BA.
Tel: 01–606–6321
Contact: J. Davis

Hambro, 41 Bishopsgate, London, EC2P 2AA.
Tel: 01–588–2851
Contact: A.R. Beevor

First Independent, Corporate Finance, 2 John Street, London, WC1N 2HJ.
Tel: 01–831–2358
Contact: John Beatty

Investors in Industry, 91 Waterloo Road, London, SE1 8XP.
Tel: 01–928–7822
Contacts: Richard Connell, John Kingston (Bristol Director)

Kleinwort Benson Development Capital, 20 Fenchurch Street, London, EC3P 3DB.
Tel: 01–623–8000
Contacts: Emrys Hughes, Alison Knocker

Managing Director, Midland Montagu Ventures Ltd, Norfolk House, 3 Laurence Pountney Hill, London, EC4R 0BP.
Contact: Dr Hugh de Quervain

The Management Buyout Association, 388–396 Oxford Street, London, W1N 9HE.
Tel: 01–491–4924
Contact: L.R. Blackstone

Pannell Kerr Forster, New Garden House, Hatton Garden, London, EC1.
Tel: 01–831–7393
Contact: Stephen Bruck

Peat, Marwick, Mitchell, 1 Puddle Dock, Blackfriars, London, EC4V 3PD.
Tel: 01–236–8000
Contact: David Carter

Philips & Drew Development Capital, Triton Court, 14 Finsbury Square, London, EC2A 1BR.
Tel: 01–628–6366
Contact: Ian Hawkins

Price Waterhouse, 32 London Bridge Street, London, SE1.
Tel: 01–407–8989
Contacts: Tom Wilson, Chris Rees

Robson Rhodes, 186 City Road, London, EC1V 2NV.
Tel: 01–251–1644
Contact: David Medland

Schroder Venture, The Schroder Group, 120 Cheapside, London EC2.
Tel: 01–382–6000
Contact: Jon Moulton

Investment Manager, Scottish Development Agency, 120 Bothwell Street, Glasgow, GW2.
Tel: 041–248–2700
Contact: Frank Gow

Simmons & Simmons (Solicitors), 14 Dominion Street, London, EC2.
Tel: 01–628–2020
Contact: Bill Knight

Simpson Curtis, 41 Park Square, Leeds, LS1 2NS.
Tel: 0532–433433
Contact: Martin Shaw

Singer & Friedlander Ltd, 21 New Street, Bishopsgate, London EC2P 2AA.
Contact: Anthony Dyaf

Appendix 4: Bibliography

'Account Guide: Management Buy-outs', *Account*, 13 March 1986.

'After the Buy-Out', *Fortune*, 9 December 1985.

'Anatomy of a Management Buy-Out', *Business Chronicle*, February, 1987.

Anslow, M. 'Warning Bells for Whizz Kids', *Business* July 1986.

Anslow, M. 'Faster Growth for Buy-out Managers', *Your Business*, July 1984.

Arnfield, V., Chipin B., Jarrett M.G., Wright D.M., *Management Buy Outs: Corporate Trend for the 80's*, IBLO, Nottingham University, 1981.

'Base for £1.5Bn Of Buy-Outs', *Venture UK*, November 1985.

Bank of Scotland 'The Changing Leveraged Buy-out Scene – The Bankers Role',

Batchelor, Charles, 'Inventive Plans for Takeovers', *Financial Times*, 8 November 1986.

Batchelor, Charles, 'Revival of the Fittest,' *Financial Times*

Blackstone, L. and Franks D., *Guide To Management Buy-Outs 1986–1987*, Economist Publications

Bevan, Judi, 'Mezzanine Puts Its Trust in Buyouts', *Sunday Times*, 30 November 1986.

Blackstone, L.R. *et al.*, 'Management Buy-Outs', special report no. 15, *Economist Intelligence Unit*, 1984.

Bradley, Keith and Gelb, Alan, 'Employee Buyouts of Troubled Companies', *Harvard*

Bruce, L., 'Parker Pens Script For Recovery', *International Management*, December 1986.

Business Review, September-October 1985.

Brown, M., 'Buy-Outs Become Big Business', *Sunday Times*, 30 November 1986.

Carter, D., 'The M.B.O. Players', Peat Marwick

Citicorp Venture Capital 'Management Leveraged Buy-Outs',

Clutterbuck, David, 'Going It Alone', *International Management*, May 1981.

Coyne, J. and Wright, M., 'Cash Flow: The Reality After The Honeymoon', *Accountancy*, April 1984.

Coyne, J. and Wright, M., 'Buy-Outs', *Lloyds Bank Review*, October 1982.

Coyne, J. and Wright, M., *Management Buy-Outs*, (London: Croom Helm 1985).

Dawkins, W., 'The Industry's High Flyer', *Financial Times* 18 December 1985.

Dawkins, W., 'Why a Buy-Out is Now a Buy-In', *Financial Times* 1986

Dawkins, W., 'When Vendors Ask Too Much', Corporate Finance 8, *Financial Times*, 3 July 1986.

Dawkins, W., 'Buy-Outs In 1985 Put At £930M', *Financial Times*, 15 July 1986.

Dawkins, W., 'Citicorp Offers Equity Finance For Buy-Outs', *Financial Times*, 22 October 1986.

Devine, Marion, 'Management Buyouts: Flushing Out The Entrepreneurs', *Manpower Policy and Practice*, Spring 1987.

Dickson, M., 'Why The Buy-Out Was Voted Out', *Financial Times*, 18 December 1985.

'Engineering A Buy-Out', *Venture UK*, September 1985.

Foreman, Tony, 'Management Buy-Outs', *Money Management*, September 1985.

Green, Sebastian, *The Meaning of Ownership in Management Buyouts*, working paper series no. 5, Centre for Business Strategy, London Business School, January 1986.

Haggett, D.S., 'Negotiating the Deal' in Arnfield, R. V. *et al.*, *Management Buy-Outs: Corporate trend for the 80's*, IBLO, Nottingham University, 1981.

Hardman, J.P. and Young, M. R., 'Management Buy-Outs', *Accounts Digest* No. 133, Spring 1983.

'Heading For The Big Buy-Out Boom', *Financial Decisions*, October 1985.

Heaford, T., 'Does it add up?', *West Business World*, November 1986.

Herzel, L. and Sherpo, R.W., 'Re-capitalisation As An Alternative To Leveraged Buy-Out', *Financial Times*, 16 April 1987.
Jackson, T., 'Cash Lessons Of A £173M Buy-Out', *Financial Times*, 15 July 1986.
Jay, John, 'Bosses Bid To Raise £156M In Top Buyout', *The Sunday Times*, 2 November 1986.
Kingston, J., 'The boom and the buyers', *Business World*, November 1986.
Lester, T., 'What the Buy-Outs Bring', *Management Today*, March 1982.
Lever, Lawrence, 'Johnson Fry Group First to Launch Best Buyout Fund' *The Times*, 3 October 1986.
Lever, Lawrence, 'Investors Are Offered Forbidden Fruits', *The Times*,
Lunch, Anthony, 'A Strategy for Growth', Management Buyins Conference, 11 March 1987, European Study Conferences Ltd.
'Management Buyouts', *Financial Times*, 10 October 1986.
'Management Buy-Out', *Money Mangement*, September 1985.
'Management Buy-Outs', *Leeds Journal*, June 1986.
'Management Buyouts', Parnell Kerr Forster, November 1986.
'Management Buy-Outs 3: Buzz Word in the City', *The Times*, 16 March 1987.
Meredith, M., 'Buyouts: The Push Behind A Growing Industry', *Scottish Business Insider-Corporate Finance*, October 1986.
Michaels, D., 'A Sale Versus A Buy-Out – The Management Dilemma', *Financial Times Supplement on Mergers and Acquisitions*, Autumn 1983.
Mills, A. and Miles P., *The Buy-Out Experience*, Spicer and Pegler, 1984.
Moulton, Jon, 'Nature and Consequences of Management Buy-Outs', Schroder Ventures at IBC Legal Studies and Services Ltd Conference, 10 June 1986.
Oakenshott, R., 'Privatization And Worker Buy-Outs', *Public Money*, December 1983.
Oates, D., 'How they made the sprays pay', *Business World*, November 1986.
Parkes, C., 'Parker tests up-market potential', *Financial Times*, 3 February 1986.
Parkes, C., 'Parker Pen halfway profit more than double forecast', *Financial Times*, 30 September 1986.

Parkes, C., 'Pen company's future rewritten', *Financial Times*, 30 October 1986.

Parker, H., 'How To Buy Out', *Management Today*, January 1986.

Peat, Marwick, Mitchell & Co., Management Buyouts And Incentive Financing', Daily Telegraph Publication, 1982.

Peat, Marwick, Mitchell & Co., 'Management Buy-Outs: How To Be Your Own Boss Without Giving Up Your Job' 1985.

'Proceedings Of The First National Conference On Management Buy-Outs', Nottingham University, 1981.

de Quervain, Hugh (Dr), 'Management Buy Ins – Setting the Scene', Management Buyins Conference, 11 March 1987, European Study Conferences Ltd.

Ridmar Marketing Research, 'Survey of Buy-Outs: *Chief Executive*, December 1982.

Rock, S., 'The image of an entrepreneur', *The Director*, May 1987.

'Sharing In, Buying Out', *Financial Times*, 8 April 1986.

Shaw, Martin, 'Company Law Implication', Simpson Curtis IBC Legal Studies and Services Ltd Conference, 'Management Buy-Outs', 10 June 1986.

Spicer & Pegler, 'The Management Buy-Out', 2nd Edition, February 1984.

Spicer & Pegler, 'The Management Buy-Out' 3rd Edition, April 1986.

Spicer & Pegler, 'The Buy-Out Experience', 1984.

Stewart, Ian, 'Buy Outs: A Do-It-Yourself Guide', *CBI News*, 7 March 1986.

'Owner-Manager Makes A Comeback', *Sunday Telegraph*, 15 May 1986

Thompson, Hugh, 'Go West Young Man', *Venture UK*, August

Upton, R., 'I'm in Personnel', *Personnel Management*, December 1983.

Walton, Michael, 'Relationship Between Management and Supporting Institutions', Electra Investment Trust at IBC Legal Studies and Services Ltd Conference, 10 June 1986.

Warner, Jeremy, 'Dramatic Rise in Buy-Outs', *The Times*, 8 April 1986.

Westmore, Geoffrey, 'The Structure Of A Management Buy-Out' Deloitte Haskins & Sells at IBC Legal Studies and Services Ltd Conference, 10 June 1986.

Webb, I., *Management Buyout. A Guide For The Prospective Entrepeneur* (Aldershot: Gower, 1985).

Williams, I., 'Why The Buy-Out', *The Sunday Times*, 24 August 1986.
Williams, I., 'Managers In Buy-Out Boom', *The Sunday Times*, 23 February 1986.

Appendix 5: What The Buyout Managers Say – A Survey

Our postal survey drew 54 responses from management teams who had achieved buyouts ranging in value from less than £100,000 to multiple millions. The response rate was approximately 30%. The questionnaire (reproduced on page 226) examined the planning they followed, the negotiation and implementation of the buyout, their attitudes during the attempt and their estimates of the buyout's success. Percentages may sometimes not add up to 100 due to rounding.

Planning the Buyout

Some 37% of the respondents cited that the opportunity for a buyout arose because their company had decided to divest its non-core activities. The retirement of the company's former owners was the second most important single factor at 15%, with poor company performance at 13%.

The motivation for the buyout was evenly spread, with overall 22% of the respondents citing their belief that they could run the company better, 21% financial gain, 20% the challenge of the situation and 18% job protection. Career advancement was a lesser interest at 12%. When asked to place these motives in order of priority, 26% gave first priority to their belief that they could run the company better, and only 10% prioritized buyouts as a method of career advancement.

In order of significance, the risks involved in a potential buyout failure were recognized by respondents to be: potential job loss (28%); the difficulty of settling back into their former jobs (24%); the damage to their personal credibility (22%); and disloyalty to the company (14%).

Implementation

When asked at what stage they sought advice for a buyout, 66% of respondents cited the virtue of seeking advice shortly after the initial plans for a buyout, 16% said that they sought advice after asking other managers to form a buyout team. 12% waited until the vendor had been informed of the intended buyout before advice was sought. With hindsight, all respondents decided that their original timing for opening up their plans to advisers was correct.

Choice of Investors and Advisers

The respondents reflected a strong desire that both advisers and investors shoud be experienced in buyouts (76%). A good rapport was the next most important quality wanted, and this was considered slightly more important in dealing with the adviser, 34%, as opposed to 30% for dealing with an investor. The general track records of investors and advisers were also important at 28% and 26% respectively. As a top priority, 49% gave importance to the investor's expertise in buyouts, and when asked about advisers, 55% prioritized their previous experience in buyouts. Only 15% of respondents gave first priority to the general track record of investors, as compared to 13% for advisers.

Generally, the survey showed that most people were happy with the performance of their advisers and investors during the course of the negotiations, but the 23% who were unhappy with their advisers' performance cited lack of buyout expertise as the main factor (38%). Frustration was also expressed at the lack of speed in decision-making on the part of the adviser (25%). Over half of those dissatisfied with the performance of their investors cited the slowness of decision-making as the major problem.

The Response

An overwhelming number of vendors, 66%, were reported to be cooperative towards the buyout offer, with only 9% overtly hostile. The others were described as surprised or indifferent.

Some 84% of the respondents personally supplied under £100,000 of the capital, with 10% raising between £100,000 and £250,000. During the course of the negotiations, 58% of the respondents experienced problems with the vendor, mostly because the vendor expected too high a price (30%) or invited other bidders (29%).

More than two thirds (69%) of the respondents found it difficult to perform well in their job while attempting the buyout, but only 17% reported outright hostility and 14% distrust and exclusion from the parent company.

The quality of the management team was described as 'crucially important' to the buyout by 76% of the respondents. The most important qualities recognized in the team were strong market knowledge (20%), intimate knowledge of the company (17%), financial skills (16%), strong leadership (15%) and entrepreneurial skills (15%). The ability to share leadership was cited by 14% of the respondents. When asked to rank in order of priority, 34% prioritized strong leadership as the most important skill for their management team, 7% prioritized entrepreneurial skills.

Relationships

To enlist the support of the workforce, 65% of the respondents had used personal presentations; 11% had promised to minimize redundancies, but only 5% used share schemes.

Not surprisingly, the closeness of the relationship with the former company decreased after the buyout. 63% described their pre-buyout relationship as close, falling to 37% after the buyout. There was a corresponding increase in the numbers of those describing their post-buyout relationship as 'indifferent' (44%). Of those who had previously had an indifferent relationship with the former owner, exactly half cited this as a contributory factor leading to the initial buyout decision. Where relations were originally indifferent, 30% said the former owner had exerted too many constraints and controls, and had not given enough support or involvement. Some 19% said that the former owner had discouraged innovation.

After the buyout, 80% of the respondents reported that they did not use their contacts in the parent company 'unofficially'.

After the Buyout

The buyouts of the survey were seen to be broadly successful, and this was reflected in increases in profits, productivity and morale.

The survey revealed that buyouts did not harm profits; 82% reported a profit increase and 18% a maintained profit. This position was reflected by the earnings per share, where 77% saw an improvement, 14% maintained their level and only 9% saw a worsening position. Productivity also saw wide improvement, with 81% of the respondents seeing productivity increase and 19% maintaining productivity at its present level.

Against this background, only 13% of the respondents said they had experienced difficulties in losing the benefits of belonging to a larger group. In three-quarters of the cases no continued support was promised from the vendor, while 10% allowed the continued use of the brand name, and only 4% allowed the use of financial services and 4% the use of administrative services. In all cases where support was promised, the vendor had given aid. Where support services had been withdrawn by the vendor, exactly half used external services, while half created new internal functions. When asked what aspects of being part of a larger group they seriously missed, 66% said none, 17% missed the technical resources and 9% the financial services.

With hindsight, most respondents felt that they had paid about the right price for the company, with only 23% feeling it was over-priced, and 17% under-priced.

Satisfaction

For the buyout teams, nearly all (94%) improved their job satisfaction through the buyout, with the remaining 6% reporting that their job satisfaction had remained the same.

The sources of the increase in job satisfaction stemmed from the freedom to make and implement decisions (27%), the greater job challenge (26%), the greater involvement (23%) and the stronger financial incentive (23%). When asked to place these sources in priority, 46% gave the freedom to make and implement decisions as their first priority, with 10% prioritizing their greater involvement.

The survey showed that 80% of respondents had fulfilled their original business plan; 18% felt they had been over-optimistic.

When asked if they thought the company was too heavily geared, 70% said no; 30% said yes.

Achievements

Some 36% cited improved efficiency as a key achievement, 27% new market penetration and 27% the development of new products.

Over half (55%) of the respondents had encountered problems with their teams, mostly because individual managers lacked competence in their new positions (39%). Almost one third (31%) felt that individuals had not pulled their weight, and 14% cited internal rivalry and jealousy as causes of problems. Against this, only 33% had changed their team since the buyout.

Customer and supplier support during the transition of ownership was widespread, with 96% reporting good support from suppliers, and 100% reporting good support from customers. Only 2% had lost suppliers and only 10% had lost customers during the course of the buyout. Of those who lost customers, 40% reported that they had since regained them, 20% had reclaimed some of them, and 40% reported that the lost customers had not come back.

Managing a Buyout – Questionnaire

Please answer the questions by ticking the boxes. When requested to list in order of priority, please insert a number, using 1 to mean the most important priority.

1) How did the opportunity for a buyout arise?

- the owners were retiring [ ]
- a division or company was performing poorly [ ]
- your company decided to divest its non-core activities [ ]
- your company was taken over and subsidiaries sold off [ ]
- Other [please specify] [ ]

2) Why did you stage a buyout? [please list in order of priority]

- to protect your job [ ]
- for career advancement [ ]
- for financial gain [ ]
- for new challenge [ ]
- because you believed you could run the division/company better [ ]
- other [please specify] [ ]

3) What did you see as the risks if the buyout should fail? [please list in order of priority]

- your action would seem disloyal [ ]
- your credibility would be damaged [ ]
- you might lose your job [ ]
- you would be unable to settle back into your former job [ ]
- other [please specify] [ ]

4) a) At what stage did you seek advice?

b) In your view, when is the best time to seek advice?

	a)	b)
• soon after thinking of a buyout	[ ]	[ ]
• after asking other managers to form a buyout team	[ ]	[ ]
• after informing your company/vendor of your intentions	[ ]	[ ]
• other [please specify]	[ ]	[ ]

5) In order of priority, what was the most important trait of your final choice of:

a) investor
b) adviser

	a)	b)
• general track record	[ ]	[ ]
• expertise in management buyouts	[ ]	[ ]
• good rapport	[ ]	[ ]
• other [please specify]	[ ]	[ ]

6) During negotiations, were you dissatisfied with the performance of your:

a) advisers
b) investors

	a)	b)
Yes	[ ]	[ ]
No	[ ]	[ ]

7) If you were dissatisfied, did your:

a) advisers
b) investors

	a)	b)
• lack expertise in buyouts	[ ]	[ ]
• act and make decisions too slowly	[ ]	[ ]
• negotiate too weakly with the vendor	[ ]	[ ]
• value the buyout too lowly	[ ]	[ ]
• attempt to gear the buyout too highly	[ ]	[ ]
• succeed in gearing the buyout too highly	[ ]	[ ]
• other [please specify]	[ ]	[ ]

8) What was the response of the vendor to the buyout offer?

- uncooperative and hostile [ ]
- indifferent [ ]
- surprised [ ]
- cooperative [ ]
- other [please specify] [ ]

9) How much capital did you personally have to supply?

- under £100,000 [ ]
- between £100,000 and £250,000 [ ]
- between £250,000 and £750,000 [ ]
- over £750,000 [ ]

10) a) During negotiations, did you experience problems with the vendor?

- yes [ ]
- no [ ]

b) If yes, did the vendor

- expect too high a price [ ]
- act and make decisions too slowly [ ]
- invite other bidders [ ]
- actively oppose the buyout [ ]
- refuse or try to suppress information [ ]
- other [please specify] [ ]

11) During the course of the buyout, did you

- experience hostility or jealousy from colleagues [ ]
- find colleagues/superiors distrusting and excluding you from business [ ]
- find it difficult to perform effectively in your job [ ]

12) How important was the quality of the management team?

- crucially important [ ]
- moderately important [ ]
- unimportant [ ]

13) How important were the following in the buyout team? [please list in order of priority]

- entrepreneurial skills [ ]
- financial skills [ ]
- a strong leader [ ]
- shared leadership qualities [ ]
- intimate knowledge of the company/division [ ]
- intimate knowledge of the market [ ]
- other [ ]

14) How did you enlist the support of the workforce?

- personal presentations [ ]
- through corporate publications [ ]
- through offering a share scheme [ ]
- through promising minimum redundancies [ ]
- other [please specify] [ ]

15) a) What were relations like with the former owner before the buyout?

b) What is the relationship like with them now?

	a)	b)
• close	[ ]	[ ]
• poor	[ ]	[ ]
• indifferent	[ ]	[ ]

16) a) If relations with the former owner were poor or indifferent, was this a contributary factor in the decision to seek a buyout?

- yes [ ]
- no [ ]

b) If relations were poor or indifferent, did the former owner:

- not give enough support or involvement [ ]
- exert too many constraints and controls [ ]
- discourage innovation [ ]
- other [please specify] [ ]

c) Do you still draw 'unofficially' on contacts in the parent company for advice?

- yes [ ]
- no [ ]

After the Buyout

1) What have been the results (both short-term and longer-term) in:

	improved	same	worsened
• profits	[ ]	[ ]	[ ]
• earnings, per share	[ ]	[ ]	[ ]
• productivity	[ ]	[ ]	[ ]
• morale	[ ]	[ ]	[ ]

2) Have you experienced difficulties because you have lost the benefits of belonging to a larger group?

• yes	[ ]	[ ]
• no	[ ]	[ ]

3) a) What continued support was promised from the vendor?

b) What aspects of being part of a larger gorup are seriously missed?

	a)	b)
• none	[ ]	[ ]
• use of brand name	[ ]	[ ]
• use of administrative services	[ ]	[ ]
• financial services	[ ]	[ ]
• marketing aid	[ ]	[ ]
• technical resources	[ ]	[ ]
• financial resources	[ ]	[ ]
• other [please specify]	[ ]	[ ]

c) If support was promised, has the vendor kept its word?

• yes	[ ]
• no	[ ]

4) If support services have been withdrawn, how have you replaced them?

• services are still waiting to be replaced	[ ]
• used external services	[ ]
• created new internal functions	[ ]

5) Do you feel you paid

a) too high a price for the company
b) too low a price for the company

	a)	b)
• yes	[ ]	[ ]
• no	[ ]	[ ]

6) a) How satisfying has it been compared with working for your former company?

- more [ ]
- same [ ]
- less [ ]

b) If your job satisfaction has increased, is this because you now have: [please list in order of priority]

- a stronger financial incentive [ ]
- greater job challenge [ ]
- freedom to make and implement decisions [ ]
- greater involvement [ ]
- other [please specify] [ ]

c) If your job satisfaction has decreased since the buyout, is this because: [please list in order of priority]

- your expectations were unrealistically high [ ]
- your company has experienced financial problems [ ]
- you are limited by financial restraints [ ]
- you have been burdened with routine administration [ ]
- other [please specify] [ ]

7) Has your business plan proved:

- fulfillable [ ]
- over-optimistic [ ]
- over-pessimistic [ ]

8) a) In hindsight, do you think the company is too heavily geared?

- yes [ ]
- no [ ]

b) Has the gearing reduced your ability to invest in necessary improvements?

- yes [ ]
- no [ ]

9) What are the key things you have achieved since the buyout?

- penetrated new markets [ ]
- developed new products [ ]
- improved efficiency [ ]
- centralized functions [ ]
- decentralized functions [ ]
- other [please specify] [ ]

10) a) Have you encountered any problems with your team?

- yes [ ]
- no [ ]

b) If you have experienced problems with your team, is this because:

- individuals have not pulled their weight [ ]
- individuals have not been competent in their new positions [ ]
- rivalry and jealousy has sprung up between individuals [ ]
- members have challenged your role as leader [ ]
- distribution of equity shares has caused ill-will [ ]

c) Have you had to change your team since the buyout?

- yes [ ]
- no [ ]

11) a) During the transition of ownership, were your:

a) suppliers supportive?
b) customers supportive?

	a)	b)
• yes	[ ]	[ ]
• no	[ ]	[ ]

12) a) Did you lose any of your:

a) suppliers
b) customers

	a)	b)
• yes	[ ]	[ ]
• no	[ ]	[ ]

c) Have they now come back?

• yes	[ ]
• some	[ ]
• no	[ ]

General Comments

Please feel at liberty to describe your experience further, or to identify points which might be of value to anyone thinking of following the same path.